Conversational competence and social development

Conversational competence and social development

Ioanna Dimitracopoulou

School of Social Sciences
University of California, Irvine

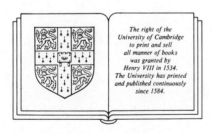

The right of the
University of Cambridge
to print and sell
all manner of books
was granted by
Henry VIII in 1534.
The University has printed
and published continuously
since 1584.

Cambridge University Press

Cambridge
New York   Port Chester
Melbourne   Sydney

Published by the Press Syndicate of the University of Cambridge
The Pitt Building, Trumpington Street, Cambridge CB2 1RP
40 West 20th Street, New York, NY 10011, USA
10 Stamford Road, Oakleigh, Melbourne 3166, Australia

First published 1990

Printed in Great Britain at the University Press, Cambridge

British Library cataloguing in publication data

Dimitracopoulou, Ioanna
  Conversational competence and social
  development.
  1. Children. Development. Role of
  acquisition of communication skills
  I. Title
  155.4'13

Library of Congress cataloguing in publication data applied for

ISBN 0 521 37551 7

To Shawn, to Angele and to Phillip,
my family

Contents

Figures

Tables

Acknowledgments

Many individuals and institutions have helped me during the eight years leading up to this book. I should like to acknowledge and thank them all.

The data could not have been collected without the cooperation of the mothers and the children who acted as my research subjects or without the help of the three California nursery schools who welcomed me. The data could not have been analyzed without the support of the London University Institute of Education, which offered technical assistance, or without the useful comments of my doctoral supervisor Angela Hobsbaum. I would also like to thank Angela for the support she gave me during all my years at the Institute.

Many other people contributed to the preparation of the book. I was first encouraged to proceed by my external examiner, Michael McTear. I also received very suggestive comments from Susan Ervin-Tripp. She devoted considerable effort to reading the manuscript. Shawn Rosenberg and Jonathan Mendilow spent hours revising several drafts. I would like to express my gratitude to them all. I should also like to thank Peter Jackson, my undergraduate tutor, for being a great teacher and a firm believer in the pursuit of new ideas. Although he did not directly contribute to this book, he made its preparation possible. Finally, there is a person I am unable to thank who always supported my academic endeavors: my father, Andreas Dimitracopoulos, who died in 1985.

1 Introducing pragmatics

Communication through the use of language is perhaps the most distinctive of human social activities. It is certainly one of the most critical. Language provides the medium through which communities are realized and reproduced through time. Whereas individuals may experience the world privately and thus construct personal definitions, their social interaction forces them to accommodate to a public and shared frame of reference. In order to ensure that one's own action is properly recognized by another and thus is likely to have its intended effect, an individual must act in accordance with rules linking intention, action and effects which are also recognized by others. It is in this public domain, this arena of commonly recognized rules, that the values, understandings and regulations of action characteristic of a community are expressed. Nowhere does this expression receive greater elaboration or clarity than in language.

Guided by a desire to better understand social life, philosophers and social scientists have focused on two questions: What does it mean for an individual to be a member of a social group? What is involved in becoming a member of such a group? Within a linguistic frame of reference these two questions may be recast as follows: What does it mean to be a competent communicator, a competent user of language? What is involved in acquiring this competence? My aim in this book is to contribute to the attempt to provide answers to these questions. To do so, I will draw on the philosophical literature which attempts to analyze the essential nature of successful communication. Guided by this, I will then present theory and empirical research on how children come to use language appropriately and thus become competent participants in conversation.

Conversation is certainly a ubiquitous and an apparently quite natural social activity. Nonetheless, the ability to converse cannot simply be assumed. Anyone who has had the experience of dealing with young children is aware that there are severe limits to their ability to participate in conversation. They are often unable to initiate conversations or to maintain the discussion of a single topic for more than a couple of conversational turns. Similarly, young children often do not say the appropriate thing at the appropriate time nor are they generally very careful about making clear what their remarks are referring to. A number of these limitations are readily apparent in the typical conversation an adult may have with a child who has just returned from a day at preschool. Queries regarding the day's events are generally met with meandering responses which wander from the topic and fail to adapt to the listener's perspective on the matters reported. As the failings of the 3- and 4-year-old would-be communicators indicate, the prevalence of conversational exchange should not lead to the assumption either of its simplicity or of the automatic and immediate ability of individuals to participate in it.

In exploring the nature of conversation, this book follows the recent efforts of those philosophers who offer a pragmatic account of the nature of language. Central to this work is the recognition that linguistic communication is not simply a matter of the specifics of what is said. Importantly, indeed essentially, it also involves the individual's attempt to act effectively in a structured social environment. To understand language, one must therefore consider how language is used. This in turn requires that one understand how the use of language is conditioned by the social context in which it is embedded.

The need to consider how language is used and to do so with reference to social context is readily illustrated by the consideration of such speech as hints or sarcasm. If one observes adults in their everyday environment, one will note how adults often conceal their intentions and communicate in indirect or non-literal ways. Consider the indirection often dictated by the rules of politeness. Take, for example, what is involved in making a request for the time of day. When you stop someone on the road, you usually say "Do you have the time?" as you are looking at his or her watch. You do this because the relevant common rule of politeness dictates that a simple and direct request such as "Tell me what time it is" is inappropriate. The other person responds by telling you what time it is because he or she is aware of the social convention you are following and thus recognizes your question "Do you have the time?" to be a request for the time. If the other person did not recognize the rule, he or she would reply to the raw semantic content of your query and tell you that he or she has the time and walk away. Similarly, the exclamation "That's great!" uttered upon dropping one's china on the floor, does not necessarily signify pleasure, but rather may convey annoyance. Indeed, one supposes that a listener will interpret the utterance in light of the circumstances and with regard to conventions of speech and thus understand it to be sarcastic.

As the foregoing examples make clear, linguistic communication is purposeful. It achieves its aims by following (or breaking) the rules of discourse and social exchange which comprise the larger culture. The question which then arises for the developmentalist is how the child develops the ability to purposively engage in social exchanges. What is it that enables the child to perceive utterances as linguistic acts, to place them in their appropriate social context, to infer the intentions that underlie them, and to understand the role they play in social interaction? It is only when the child is able to do all of this that his or her communication with others will be successful. This ability to understand and use language develops gradually. To begin with, the sentences he or she uses involve simple objects and events which are located in his/her immediate environment. Eventually, the child must enter into a more public world. He or she must possess the concepts that the adult community shares and recognize other people's points of view. Communication through language helps the child to see others as people who have their own wants and intentions yet share a common form of life and mode of linguistic expression. With time, the understanding of personal intentions, conversational conventions, and social knowledge expands and new linguistic and social concepts are formed to orient communication in various contexts and social situations.

This book offers a careful pragmatic analysis of the functions language can perform and an empirical investigation of the development of the young child's communicative skills. Both parts of the inquiry are pre-dicated on the understanding that the effective use of language depends on an awareness of both the perspective of the hearer and the social context in which the conversation is occurring. In this respect, it is assumed that language use and general social cognition are closely related to one another. Thus the book supplements the empirical investigation of children's language use with an examination of their socio-cognitive abilities and analyzes the links between the two.

The pragmatic point of view

Pragmatics focuses on how language is used in a social context. It does so in recognition of the fact that the meaning of utterances depends as much on their use as on their specific semantic content. An appropriate understanding of this meaning depends on both. The earlier discussion of asking for the time or responding to one's broken china provides examples of this. In both cases, the appropriate decoding of the meaning of the speaker's utterances requires a consideration of the semantic content of the utterance with regard to the immediate context and the relevant social conventions of how language may be used. A further example is provided by Levinson (1983). Consider the following sentences:

(1)   Getting married and having a child is better than having a child and getting married.
(2)   Having a child and getting married is better than getting married and having a child.

Clearly, sentence 1 does not have the same meaning as sentence 2. However, there is no difference in the purely semantic meaning of the two sentences. Nonetheless, we attribute different meaning to each. We do so because we employ a pragmatic principle governing the reporting of events which dictates that we report the events in the order in which they usually occur. An example of a different way in which linguistic meaning is pragmatically constituted is provided by words such as "well," "indeed," and "oh." A moment's reflection makes clear how the explication of the meaning of these words necessarily entails a consideration of the intentions and social conventions related to their use.

With its focus on the function and social context of language, the pragmatic study of language constitutes a reaction to more traditional treatments of language, in which it is conceived in more mentalistic and subjective terms. This more abstract conception of language is evidenced in a variety of forms from the classical statements of John Locke through the more recent work of Noam Chomsky. What these various approaches share is the presumption of a radical separation between the words in which thoughts are expressed and the thoughts themselves. The latter belong to a world of mental experience which is essentially personal and individual. In this private world, meaning is said to be the product of a number of mental acts or processes which underlie the intelligent use of language. In simple terms, words stand for or refer to inner processes of thought. The medium in which thought occurs consists of images and ideas. Initially the simple representations of an external reality, these images and ideas can through reflection be refined and combined to produce more complex concepts.

Beginning with Wittgenstein and continuing with Austin and Searle, the pragmatic philosophy of language has emerged in part as a critique of this abstract conception of meaning in terms of mental entities which may be defined quite apart from the uses and users of language. For example, a question commonly posed is: How would it be possible to form a concept by reflection on the common features of experience, when the recognition of those common features is only possible after one has already established the criteria for determining whether a given experience constitutes an instance or example of the concept to be formed? If a child sees a tree and, on reflecting on its common features, comments "This is a tree," then the child must have already established the concept of "treeness" in order to recognize the tree as such. In light of basic conundrums such as this, pragmatic philosophers have moved towards the view that meaning can be understood only in terms of the speaker's beliefs and intentions as they direct acts of communication in specific contexts of social interaction.

As an ordinary language philosopher, Wittgenstein (1958) began to chart the features of everyday discourse in terms of patterns known as "language games." He demonstrated how slight and subtle changes in the use of language would alter its meaning; hence the plea "Don't ask for the meaning, ask for the use." In this vein, he argued that assigning names to objects was preliminary to the use of language and not an example of it. In *Philosophical Investigations*, he claims: "Naming is not so far a move in the language game any more than putting a piece in its place on the board is a move in chess" (1958, p. 6). In this light, learning to attach labels to certain objects does not constitute understanding, but rather is simply a process of copying and repetition. Indeed, in many cases the correct labeling of an object depends on an understanding which goes beyond the available perceptual evidence, one which shows how the object is implicated in life situations or social interactional contexts. The pedagogical consequences of this view of language are clear. We teach children new words by encouraging them to learn their application in appropriate situations rather than by encouraging them to conjure up mental images, acquired or innate.

Seen in this light, language is a form of social action. In John Searle's terms, the study of language consists of the study of speech-acts. A speech-act is characterized by the speaker's specific intention to produce an effect on the audience. In this sense, linguistic communication involves human agency and the meaning of a speech-act is defined by the actor's definition of his or her own line of action. At the same time, a speech-act achieves its end of producing an effect on an audience by means recognized by the audience to be associated with the intention to produce the desired effect. In this latter regard, linguistic communication occurs in the context of structured interpersonal exchange and meaning is thus socially regulated. To understand language, both these aspects must be considered together. Meanings are produced by personal intentions and intentions are defined by social conventions of meaningful expression.

In my view, linguistic communication is fruitfully regarded as a problem-solving exercise. A speaker, qua communicator, has to solve the problem: Given that I want to create a particular effect in the hearer's consciousness what is the best way to accomplish this aim? For the hearer, the complementary problem must be solved: given that the speaker has made a particular statement, what did he or she intend me to understand by it? It is important to recognize that the participants are able to reach solutions only insofar as each presumes the other is acting in a way constrained by certain principles of "good communicative behavior." It is because both speaker and hearer presume that the other is conforming to social conventions regarding language use in their own particular exchange that each is able to solve his or her part of the problem posed by their communication.

Language acquisition and social development

Viewed from a pragmatic perspective, language is an essentially social and active entity. It is a communicative activity in which intention, dialogue, group interaction and social context are significant for understanding. Words acquire their meaning as people use them to achieve ends in socially regulated ways. Given this perspective, language acquisition must be seen as critically linked to the growth of effective social functioning. To learn to speak a language, a child must do more than learn its grammatical and semantic rules. The child must also acquire knowledge of how the adult community uses language and how that use structures social life. He or she must become able to discern the relevant context of discourse: what is assumed, what must be made clear and what is conversationally implied. In so doing, the child must not only have a clear intention to produce an effect on the hearer, but must also understand that other persons may have a different perspective and different intentions from his or her own.

Viewing language in these terms, there are several questions which developmentalists must address to provide an initial focus to their inquiry. These are: (1) What sorts of behavior should be regarded as linguistic and hence a proper focus of study? (2) What are the general requirements of successful linguistic communication? (3) How do the foregoing requirements come to be met by the developing child? The first question delineates the descriptive boundaries of the research. The second establishes its normative parameters. These two questions thus pose issues which are essentially theoretical. A number of different models addressing these questions have been put forward by philosophers to account for various aspects of linguistic communication. Some of the most important of these are introduced and extended in chapter 2. The third and final question defines a research agenda for developmental psychology. Guided by the definitions constructed in response to the theoretical questions, it becomes the developmental psychologist's task to conduct empirical research to establish how linguistic development proceeds. My own efforts here are presented in chapters 4 and 5.

My aim in the book is to provide a fairly comprehensive exploration of the child's developing use of language. The focus is on his or her emerging ability to use and understand speech-acts and to engage cooperatively in conversations. Three topics of concern are examined in depth:

(1) The development of direct and indirect speech-acts. The goal here is to understand how the child learns to master the linguistic forms and social conventions which regulate the use of utterances. Emphasis is thus on language use as a social act which is performed in specific contexts.

(2) The development of communicative behaviors. Here the interest is in understanding how the child comes to monitor his or her participation in conversation by taking into account the perspective of his or her interlocutors and the guiding value of cooperation.

(3) The development of social inferential abilities. The focus is on those cognitive abilities necessary for understanding conversationally implied meanings. Of particular interest is how the child is able to use his or her knowledge of others and the world when using language or when decoding the language of others.

Throughout, my inquiry is informed by the recognition that language is an aspect of social life and must be understood accordingly. As a result, the investigation of linguistic development is supplemented by an examination of those aspects of social cognition which are central to the development of communicative competence. The relationship between language and social functioning is examined in some detail in chapter 3. The results of my empirical investigation of the relationship between the growth of specific socio-cognitive skills on the one hand and the emergence of different types of speech-acts and conversational abilities on the other is reported in chapter 6.

Following this course, I hope to broaden the study of child language development. On the one hand, I attempt to supplement recent efforts to study language development with a comprehensive pragmatic analysis of language use. On the other hand, I attempt to broaden the scope of this pragmatically oriented research by investigating the child's social know-ledge. Others have suggested the need to move in this direction (e.g. Ervin-Tripp, 1978a, 1979; Ochs, 1979). None, however, have actually done so. By carefully examining this relationship between conversational competence and social development, I not only attempt to forward the basic analysis of language. I also draw on the results and, in the final chapter of the book, suggest a new frame of reference within which to analyze language disorders and to design clinical interventions.

2 Toward an elaborated model of language: speech-act theory and conversational analysis

I have argued that language is best understood as a system of communication and that the meaning of a term is most appropriately explicated by an account of what can be done with it. This conception of language and meaning leads to a view of children's language development that focuses on how children use language in order to communicate. Thus far, the argument has been presented in very general terms. It remains to develop a model of language which is sufficiently elaborated to serve as a guide for the study of child language.

With the aim of presenting a model of child language, the chapter begins with a discussion of the philosophy of speech-acts. As a comprehensive attempt to analyze the communicative functions performed by language, it offers various typologies of speech activity which may guide the description of children's language usage. A careful consideration of speech-act theory, however, suggests that the functions utterances perform can only be fully understood by considering how these utterances are positioned in the context of particular language games or conversations. This leads to a discussion of issues in the analysis of conversation in the second part of the chapter. When conversing, people interact in a variety of ways, they employ a variety of strategies for realizing their intentions, and they draw on a pool of shared background knowledge in order to understand one another. The consideration of these dimensions of conversational exchange complements the preceding analysis of speech-acts. The result is an analytical framework for the study of language which offers both a comprehensive and a well-differentiated view of the communicative uses to which language is put. The framework has two components: a speech-act component and a component for conversational meaning. The chapter ends with a discussion of the relevance of this framework to the study of child language. It offers the basis for a careful analysis of the different forms which communicative linguistic behavior may take and provides a clear definition of the end toward which language development moves. In so doing, it also defines the aims which should guide the study of children's language and its development. They are (1) to understand how children become competent conversational partners, (2) to determine how children learn to carry out the full spectrum of speech-acts, and (3) to discover what levels of conversational competence and what kinds of speech-acts are characteristic of children at different development levels.

Speech-act theory

A key question to be confronted in the study of language as a communicative activity relates to the sort of behavior linguistic behavior is. This leads to analysis of what "speakers do with words" and how people relate words to the world. Of all attempts to deal with these issues, speech-act theory has aroused the widest interest. Psychologists have suggested that the acquisition of the concepts underlying speech-acts may be a prerequisite for the acquisition of language in general (e.g. Bruner, 1975; Bates, 1976). Literary critics have looked to speech-act theory for an illumination of textual subtleties or for an understanding of the nature of literary genres (e.g. Levin, 1976), and philosophers have seen potential application to, among other things, the status of ethical statements (e.g. Searle, 1969). This interest has been partly aroused because speech-act theory is the only one so far to attempt to formulate models of "how" to deal with such relevant subjective phenomena as a speaker's intentions and a hearer's shareable assumptions about the world. It suggests that language use is governed by a system of public rules and criteria capable of being stated. Importantly, these rules may be investigated empirically by observing language as it is used in identifiable socio-linguistic contexts. With regard to the study of language acquisition and development, speech-act theory forces us to take into account two main parameters of children's language: (a) the child's intentions in communicating with others, and (b) the context of intersubjectivity or shared understandings within which speech-acts occur.

J. L. Austin (1962) noted that some sentences, like "I object" or "I apologize," are not used merely to say things (i.e. describe states of affairs), but also to do things. Isolating such utterances, he termed them "performatives" and contrasted them to statements, assertions and utterances, which he called "constatives." Whereas constatives are utterances assessed in terms of truth and conditions, performatives are utterances assessed in terms of felicity conditions. The latter are the conditions which performatives must meet if they are to succeed or be "happy." Austin distinguished three main requisites of felicity: (1) there must be a conventional procedure which applies, and the persons and circumstances must conform to the requirements of that procedure; (2) the conventional procedure must be executed correctly and completely; and (3) the people involved must have the thoughts and intentions required by the procedure. The importance of these requisites is readily illustrated by a case where any one of them is not fulfilled. Consider the example of a host welcoming an arriving guest by mistakenly addressing the taxi driver (violating the first requisite), of a priest baptizing a baby with the wrong name (violating the second requisite), or of a young man amorously addressing a woman who does not share his view of their relationship (violating the third requisite). In each of these examples, the lack of the requisite felicity conditions seriously compromises the prospects for a successful communication.

A major shift in Austin's work followed his realization that his original distinction between constatives and performatives was not exhaustive and that one could in fact consider a whole family of speech-acts of which constatives and performatives were only particular members. Austin began by expanding the class of performatives to include implicit as well as explicit performatives. The utterance "Go," for example, may perform an advice or an order – doing, entreating or daring according to context. However, simple statements or constatives were omitted. The question then arose as to whether such statements were really different. Could they too have a performative aspect? Once the doubt was raised a few observations readily confirmed the insubstantial nature of the performative–constative dichotomy. For example, there is clearly no real incompatibility between utterances being truth-bearers and performing actions at one and the same time. Thus "I warn you the gun may fire" seems both to perform the action of warning and to issue a prediction which can be assessed as true or false. Austin consequently came to reject the dichotomy between performatives and constatives in favor of a more general theory of speech-acts.

At this point, Austin recognized that if the claim that in uttering a sentence one is also doing things was to be meaningfully advanced, it would be necessary to specify the ways in which one might be said to be performing actions by saying something. Following this imperative, he distinguished three kinds of acts that are performed simultaneously:

(1) Locutionary act: the utterance of a sentence with determinate sense and reference.
(2) Illocutionary act: the making of a statement, an offer, a promise, etc. by virtue of the conventional force associated with the sentence.

(3) Perlocutionary act: the bringing-about of effects on the audience by means of uttering the sentence, such effects being special to the circumstances of utterance.

To illustrate these distinctions, consider the example of the utterance, "I'll kill you." The locutionary act is one of stipulating a certain action, who will perform it and to whom it will be directed. The illocutionary act is that of threatening the addressee. Finally, the perlocutionary act is that of actually inducing fear in the addressee. It is the second kind of act, the illocutionary act, that became the focus of further work. Indeed, the term "speech-act" came to refer exclusively to that kind of act.

The next major contribution in this area was made by John Searle. In an attempt to further develop the analysis of illocutionary acts, Searle (1976) proposed that there are five basic kinds of action-carrying utterances:

(1) Representatives: utterances which commit the speaker to the truth of the expressed proposition (paradigm cases: asserting, concluding).
(2) Directives: utterances which are attempts by the speaker to get the addressee to do something (paradigm cases: requesting, questioning).
(3) Commissives: utterances which commit the speaker to some future action (paradigm cases: promising, threatening, offering).
(4) Expressives: utterances which express a psychological state (paradigm cases: thanking, apologizing, welcoming, congratulating).
(5) Declarations: utterances which effect immediate changes in the institutional state of affairs and which tend to rely on elaborate extra-linguistic institutions (paradigm cases: declaring war, christening, firing from employment).

Searle's typology provides a much more differentiated view of speech-acts. Offering detailed descriptions for each language function has clear advantages for the study of child language development. Guided by such a model, we can detect the different functions that the child at different developmental periods performs with language. We can isolate the "form" from the "function" of an utterance and see how the child gradually learns to use the same form to perform various functions. For example, it has been suggested that some speech-acts are far more complicated than others and require semantic and syntactic complexity to be carried out and realized as such (Dore, 1979; McShane, 1980). In particular, commissives are sophisticated language uses. They require fairly specific conversational uses of words to realize their intentions. If this is so, applying Searle's model enables us to see what acts develop at what age and what they require. In so doing, it expands our knowledge of the conditions required for speech-acts to be realized and successfully carried out.

Although Searle's typology represents an important advance and has been interestingly applied to the study of children's language use, it is nonetheless subject to several significant criticisms. Together, they suggest a need to go beyond an isolated analysis of speech-acts to one which incorporates an analysis of the conversational context in which speech-acts occur. To begin with, there is the criticism persuasively levied by Levinson (1983) that Searle's typology lacks a principled basis. Such a basis could have been built through a systematic analysis of the felicity conditions which speech-acts must meet if they are to succeed. In other words, the differentiation of speech-acts could have been systematically linked to an analysis of the conversational context in which they occur. Despite Searle's claims to the contrary, his typology is not grounded in this way. Consequently, there is no reason to believe it to be definitive or exhaustive. Applying the typology to the study of the child's development, we can never be sure whether the lack of certain speech-acts can be attributed to the child's immaturity with respect to the actual language system or to the child's problems in appreciating the conversational context and the various conditions that his or her acts must meet.

A second criticism focuses on the quality of the distinctions Searle does make. Like Austin, Searle distinguished between illocutionary and perlocutionary acts in terms of what is done *in* saying something and what is done *by* saying something. This, however, does not help us understand the differences between illocutionary and perlocutionary acts. The problem here is that the distinction made is not explained or carefully defended. Strawson (1964) suggested that effective illocutionary acts require the hearer's recognition of the speaker's intention. The speaker intends the hearer to identify the very act he intends to perform and successful communication requires fulfillment of that intention. But if this is the case, then, generally speaking, we cannot rely, as Searle did, on our vocabulary of verbs of action to differentiate illocutionary and perlocutionary acts. The issue here is critical, since it raises a new concern which fundamentally denies the appropriateness of Searle's basic approach. If we build on Strawson's claim regarding the effectiveness of illocutionary acts, it is apparent that shared social conventions are integral to the sense and possibility of these speech-acts. More importantly, this is to suggest that "meaning" itself is a matter of convention.

The foregoing line of argument leads to a recognition of the role of convention and context in meaningful communication. While true, this must be tempered by an appreciation of the full complexity and creativity of linguistic exchange. Meaning is as much a matter of people's communicative intentions as it is a matter of their shared conventions. As Grice (1975) put it, meaning presupposes the idea of people meaning things in a social context. Furthermore, for X to have meant anything, not merely must it have been uttered with the intention of inducing a certain belief, but also the speaker must have intended an audience to recognize the intention behind the utterance. Thus, to summarize Grice's point of view, "A meant something by X" is roughly equivalent to A uttered X with the intention of inducing a belief by means of the recognition of this intention. As soon as we introduce the concept of intention as being of vital importance for linguistic communication, then we need a model which directly addresses the *inferential* process that the hearer undertakes in discovering his partner's communicative intentions at each point of their linguistic communication. It is the intentional element in communicative exchanges that enables one to understand not only synonymous or ambiguous utterances but also non-literal and indirect performances of illocutionary acts. For example, consider a husband's stating to his wife "It's eight o'clock." Such a remark might simply be a direct reference to the time or it might be an indirect warning that it is late and that they should be going. Here the speaker's meaning can only be determined with reference to his intention.

Building on Grice's theory of communicative intention, Bach and Harnish (1979) have constructed their own taxonomy of speech-acts. They have argued that there are five types of utterances: constatives, directives, commissives, expressives, and acknowledgments. Although quite similar to Searle's taxonomy, it improves on his effort because the categorization of utterances is made with reference to their place in the overall communicative context. Particular attention is paid to the nature of the intentions underlying those utterances and the kinds of effects they are to achieve in the recipients. The conjunction of intentions and effects are then analyzed with reference to general considerations of the principles guiding human conduct, most centrally rationality and cooperation. This then provides a basis for the analysis of the felicity conditions of each major type of illocutionary act.

Any analysis of speech-acts is confronted by a problem of correct interpretation. As any attempt to empirically investigate speech-acts would immediately make apparent, language is "rich" in meanings. Woven into the social context of an exchange, language has great power and flexibility.

Both adults and children can use utterances to perform a variety of functions. Thus language can operate on several levels at the same time. For example, the child's classic utterance, "mommy sock" (Bloom, 1973), can be seen both as a statement of a proposition conveying the speaker's attitude (i.e. "This is mommy's sock") and as a device used to control the discourse and constrain the listener's behavior (i.e. "This is mommy's sock and you shouldn't touch it"). Interpretation will depend to a great degree on the assumptions the listener will share with the child, his or her interpretation of the child's intention, and the context of the child's utterance. Consequently, to analyze even conversational moves as apparently simple as this one needs a model of linguistic communication such as that provided by Bach and Harnish – that is, a model which attempts to account for the *context* of our utterances together with our *interpretative* processes, whereby we understand the intentions behind each other's utterances.

Firmly believing that meaning must be seen in terms of conventional as well as intentional behavior, Bach and Harnish devised a model for speech-act communication which takes into account contextual information. Given that the realization of the utterance's meaning depends, at least partially, on the realization of the speaker's intentions, one obvious problem is how to arrive at a model of linguistic communication which attempts to decode the speaker's communicative intentions. They proposed a model which offers an account of the way the hearer identifies the expression uttered, the meaning it has in the language, what the speaker means by it, and to what things he is referring. Once the hearer identifies these various items, he has identified what is said. This, together with certain mutual contextual beliefs, allows the hearer to proceed to the identification of the speaker's illocutionary act. Bach and Harnish's schematization of this identification and inference is called a speech-act schema. Their intention and inference approach contrasts sharply with Austin's view of illocutionary acts as conventional and with Searle's notion of constitutional rules (i.e. the rules that create or constitute the activity itself, like, for example, the rules that create the activity of warning someone).

Following Bach and Harnish (1979) the different aspects of a speech-act are:

Utterance act: S utters E.
Locutionary act: S says to hearer that so-and-so is the case.
Illocutionary act: S does such-and-such in communicating E.
Perlocutionary effect: S affects the hearer in a certain way.

These acts are intimately related. The achievement of the perlocutionary effects depends on the hearer identifying each of the other acts.

The speech-act schema proposed by Bach and Harnish is an inferential one. It focuses on the process whereby adults understand direct, indirect, literal, and non-literal expressions. The inference the hearer makes is based not just on what the speaker says. It is also based on certain "mutual contextual beliefs" and on three presumptions which are shared not just between the speaker and hearer, but by the members of the linguistic community at large. These three presumptions are:

(1) The linguistic presumption: members of the linguistic community share a common language (L) and whenever any member S utters E in L to any other member H, H can identify what S is saying, given that H knows the meaning(s) of E in L and is aware of the appropriate background information.

(2) The communicative presumption: whenever a member S says something E to another member H, he is doing so with some recognizable illocutionary intent.

(3) The presumption of literalness: the belief in the linguistic community that whenever any member S utters any E in L to any other member H, if S could (under the circumstances) be speaking literally, then S is speaking literally. If it is evident to H that S could not be speaking literally, H supposes S to be speaking non-literally and seeks to identify what that non-literal illocutionary act is.

Some elaboration of the schema is in order. The locutionary act, the act of saying something, provides the hearer with the core of information from which to infer the speaker's illocutionary (communicative) intent. Even when the speaker (S) speaks literally, such that his illocutionary intent is made more or less explicit by what he says, his intent has to be inferred by the hearer. According to Bach and Harnish, this inference works as follows.

S utters expression E.

1(a) E means . . . in Language (L).	Basis: Hearer (H) hears S uttering E. H has knowledge of L (linguistic presumption).
2(b) S means . . . by E.	Assuming the existence of the linguistic presumption, H understands E.

Hearer H at 1(a) of the SAS (speech-act schema) realizes that S has uttered

E. Assuming S meant anything at all by E, to reach 2(b) H must determine what S meant by E, that is the operative meaning of E. However, in as much as ambiguity is rampant in natural languages, H is likely to need more than the linguistic presumption and the identity of E to determine what S meant by E. He would need to reject all but one of the meanings of E as contextually inappropriate and rely on certain mutual contextual beliefs to do this. Accordingly, his inference would take the following form:

S is uttering E, "Let's start."

Inference		*Basis for inference*
1(a)	E means "Let's start" in L.	H hears S utter E and has knowledge of L (linguistic presumption).
(b)	S means "Let's start" by E.	Communicative presumption.
(c)	The literal meaning of E is contextually appropriate.	Mutual contextual belief: the speaker and the hearer are just about to start a basketball game.
2(b)	S means "Let's start" (let's play) by expression E.	

It should be noted that Bach and Harnish do not claim that contextual selection always represents a psychologically real process nor do they argue that selection necessarily proceeds in the precise sequence specified.

As illustrated by the preceding example, the Bach and Harnish analysis highlights two essential features of linguistic communication: (1) any communicative exchange involves interpretative activity on the part of the participants; (2) utterances occur in a particular social context and the participants' interpretation of those utterances depends on that context. This in turn suggests that in the study of language development, we need to concentrate not only on the literal meaning of an utterance, but also on the meaning this utterance may acquire by virtue of its position in a specific conversational context (i.e. its conversational meaning). In other words, we need to concentrate on the way children "learn to mean" by using words in social contexts and by performing speech-acts. However, the study of speech-acts cannot be made rigid. The understanding of speech-acts is based not on a set of *ad hoc* conventional rules but rather on a set of principles of inference regarding the interlocutor's communicative intentions in specific contexts. Thus, in coding the child's speech-act as a request or a warning, the investigator might employ Bach and Harnish's model, which acknowledges the need to make certain inferences concerning the context, the other's intentions and linguistic conventions.

Regardless of the specific model employed, the analysis of speech-acts would benefit enormously by a consideration of conversations and conversational behavior. This would be specially true if models of conversational behavior can provide us with a general theory of the nature of interpersonal interactions. Then a framework of analysis which combines a speech-act analysis with an analysis of the actual properties of natural conversations could bridge the obvious gap between speech-act categorization and actual dialogue.

Analysis of conversational exchange

"Conversation" is considered to be the most important dynamic context of language. It consists of "that familiar predominant kind of talk in which two or more participants freely alternate in speaking which generally occurs outside specific institutional settings, like religious institutional settings, law courts, classrooms and the like" (Levinson, 1983, p. 284). Although it is stipulated that conversations must occur outside of institutionally regulated settings, this is not to imply that conversations are structureless activities. Clearly, there are certain requirements which must be met if the message being sent and the intentions of the speaker sending it are to be understood. Utterances must be organized so that they are consistent with various social conventions. They must be relevant to the general topic and account for the fact that a listener might need extra information for sufficient comprehension of the speaker's intention. In addition, the people making the utterances must have some means of regulating their interaction. For example, there must be some way of determining when it is time for one person to cease talking and for another to begin. Taken together these considerations suggest that conversational behavior has structure. It is governed by rules which regulate the generation and interpretation of speech, the report of beliefs about practices, and the standards for correctness. The implication for the student of child language is clear. He or she must determine *how* the rules of conversation and address can be discovered and adequately stated, and then explain how the child acquires and develops these rules.

One prominent approach to the analysis of the rules of conversation has been developed by ethnomethodologists (e.g. Sacks *et al.*, 1974; Pomerantz, 1983). Their approach is essentially empirical. It begins with the observation and recording of many naturally occurring conversations. These records are then carefully reviewed in the hope of discovering recurring patterns to the exchanges. The aim is to build on this to determine inductively what the systematic properties of conversation are whereby utterances are structured to manage conversational sequences. An example of the result of adopting this ethnomethodological approach is the discovery that conversation is characterized by turn-taking and that 5% of the speech stream is delivered in overlap (i.e. two speakers speaking simultaneously). Building on this base, an attempt has been made to understand what mechanisms govern turn-taking, how speakers signal that their turn is over and some other party is invited to speak next, and how "adjacency-pairs" (i.e. questions–answers, greeting–greeting) manage organization in conversation. Whereas turn-taking and adjacency-pair organization are usually thought of as referring to local organization (in the sense that they operate in the first instance across just two turns), there are also quite different orders of organization in conversation. In particular, there are certain recurrent kinds of sequences for which one can derive a ranking set of sequence types. For example, a summons is usually followed by a turn which justifies the summons:

    Ch: Mummy.
    M: Yes, dear.
    Ch: I want a cloth to clean [the] windows.

(Atkinson and Drew, 1979, p. 46)

Although the work of the ethnomethodologists is interesting, it has led to little research on the development of conversational skills. The reason for this is simple. The focus of the ethnomethodological work is on the management of conversations. This social and interactive quality of conversation is understood in its own terms, that is without reference to any general or inherent qualities of individuals. To the degree to which individuals are considered, they are viewed as the subjects of regulation and hence shaped by the conditions of their interaction. In this context, the analysis of conversations is not framed in light of the *reciprocal* determination of conversational structures and the cognitive capacities of the individuals involved. Consequently, questions regarding the ways in which conversations impose cognitive requirements on the individuals involved and the ways in which the cognitive capacities of individuals delimit the quality of the conversations in which they can engage are not addressed.

A second approach to the analysis of conversation has been developed by Grice (1975). Adopting an essentially theoretical approach, he offers a deductive analysis of how people cooperate for the efficient use of language. His aim is to understand and codify the pragmatic rules for the conversational use of language. To do so, Grice attempts to isolate those principles or strategies upon which individuals must depend if they are to arrive at inferences regarding the intentions an interlocutor has in saying what he or she says.[1]

According to Grice, all conversations have three characteristics. The first is that they occur against a background of shared knowledge and assumptions (e.g. speaker and hearer share a common language). This requires little elaboration at this point. The second characteristic is that the utterances exchanged have a conversational as well as a literal meaning. The distinction between these two meanings is important. Indeed, it is one of the key contributions to the study of language made by pragmatics. A recognition of conversational implicature provides the basis for an explicit account of how it is possible to mean more than what is actually "said" (i.e. more than what is literally expressed by the conversational sense of the linguistic expression uttered). For example, consider the following:

A: Has Phillip left?
B: There's a BMW outside the house.

All that we can reasonably expect a semantic theory to tell us about this minimal exchange is that there is at least one reading that we might paraphrase as follows:

A: Do you have the ability to tell whether Phillip has left?
B: A BMW is parked outside the house. (An irrelevant response)

Yet it is clear to native speakers that what would ordinarily be communicated by such an exchange involves considerably more:

A: Do you have the ability to tell me whether Phillip has left?
B: No, I didn't see him going, but I can provide some information from which you may be able to deduce whether Phillip has left, namely his car, which happens to be a BMW, is still here.

An important issue that emerges as soon as one concentrates on conversational meaning is how children understand not only the "literal" meaning of X but also the conversationally implied or conveyed meaning of X. To answer this question, one has to introduce Grice's third characteristic of conversations, that the messages conveyed in a conversation have a *cooperative* function (i.e. they are an integral part of a jointly entered activity intending to make sense). The claim here is that cooperation between partners is of crucial importance for their interpretation of what each is saying to the other. Analyzing the nature of this aspect of conversation, Grice (1975) spelled out certain elements of cooperation ("Be relevant," "Be clear," "Contribute only the information needed") and argued that participants in a conversation actively assume each other's cooperation. Thus they assume that contributions are relevant and are intended to follow from verbal prompts and/or from the situational context. It is this assumption that allows speakers and hearers to go beyond the literal meanings of utterances to an understanding of the meanings intended. For example, the utterance "I'll close the window" in response to a statement "It's cold in here" can be understood as a true response to the speaker's statement only when the hearer assumes the maxim of relevancy. Similarly, the response "There is a BMW parked outside the house" is relevant to the question of whether Phillip has left because it is cooperative with it at some deeper level. By assuming cooperation the hearer forces himself or herself to find the connection between the location of a BMW and Phillip himself.

It is immediately apparent that the work of Bach and Harnish has been deeply influenced by Grice. Consequently, their analysis of language attempts to elucidate the process whereby people come to terms with and comprehend many complex instances of speech such as indirect or non-literal utterances. Consider the following exchange:

> A: I am willing to be patient.
> B: The door is over there!

Here, speaker A makes a declaration of his willingness to go on cooperating with his partner. However, hearer B responds with an utterance that one might classify to begin with as irrelevant. The utterance B produces is a statement which in terms of semantic or grammatical analysis of the exchange cannot be considered as a follow-up of A's utterance. But when we analyze the above exchange with a pragmatic approach in mind, we begin with the recognition that both A and B are involved in an argument. A is willing to be more patient and somehow to start the interaction from the beginning. B, however, is unwilling to do so. He chooses an indirect speech-act to inform his partner that it is time for him to go. When applied to complicated speech-acts such as this, Bach and Harnish's analysis is as follows:

> L1 S is uttering E.
>   (a) S means "The door is over   Linguistic presumption: both H
>   there" by E in L.   and S assume knowledge of L
>   (Language).

(b) S means "The door is over there."	Contextual information: a statement concerning the whereabouts of a door is not the issue of the present context of discourse.
(c) The supposition that S means "The door is over there" by E is inappropriate given the context.	Communicative presumption: speaker A cannot *merely* mean E. Mutual contextual beliefs: (i) both participants are having a fight; (ii) doors are used for the purposes of entering or leaving.
L2 S means "The door is over there and you should leave the room" by E.	The interpretation is contextually relevant.

The model of "conversation" that is adopted here provides a theory of interpersonal relations. For conversation to take place, both participants must behave according to certain maxims. Both must observe the "cooperative" maxim, make contributions which are relevant and have an intention to communicate. These are, therefore, general features of linguistic communication connected with general patterns of human activity.

Applications to the study of child language

Thus far I have attempted to elaborate the pragmatic philosophical claim that language is best considered in terms of the communicative uses to which it is put. This led first to a consideration of speech-act theory and the taxonomy of functions which utterances can perform. Focusing on the relatively sophisticated model of Bach and Harnish, it became apparent that the analysis of speech-acts had to be supplemented by a consideration of their place in conversations. This in turn led to examination of the nature of conversations themselves and the demands they place on the individuals engaged in them. Thus the analytical framework that I suggest for the study of child language has two components. First, the child's language should be studied in terms of the functions it performs in specific social contexts. At the same time, the same speech-act should be viewed against the background of conversational participation. Having sketched an analytical framework for the study of language, it is now necessary to specify the direction this establishes for the empirical study of child language development. My own research follows this direction.

Speech-acts

As suggested earlier, a key contribution of speech-act theory is the taxonomy of speech-acts that it offers. Thus it offers empirical research categories of language behavior to investigate. The implications of this for child language are, at least at one level, straightforward. The aim of research becomes one of discovering the types of language behavior the child engages in at various stages in his development. However, the consideration of speech-acts in the context of child development adds another dimension to the analysis, which has hitherto been insufficiently examined by philosophers. Whereas in the case of adults, the ability to perform the full spectrum of speech-acts may be assumed (although even here the warrant for the assumption is unclear), in the case of children, it cannot. Consequently, in the analysis of language development, a new and central theoretical issue arises: What are the cognitive and social abilities that are required for the performance of different kinds of speech-acts? This question requires an analysis which attempts to integrate two research enterprises which have proceeded on surprisingly separate lines, that of the study of language development and that of the study of social development. The goal of such an integrative analysis would be to provide the theoretical guidance needed to understand fully the fruits of empirical research, that is the sequence in which different kinds of speech-acts are observed to become part of the developing child's communicative repertoire.

The recognition that the socio-linguistic capacities of the child are different at different stages in his or her development raises a second concern which the study of child language may profitably address. The issue here is the consequences of the child's developing abilities for the kinds of social interactions in which he or she can participate. Clearly, insofar as the child is able to perform and comprehend different kinds of speech-acts, and thus express and infer different kinds of illocutionary intent, he or she will be able to engage in more flexible and sophisticated forms of social interaction. Consequently, one interesting avenue that may be explored is the ways in which speech-acts are embedded in the context of the mother–child interaction. By examining the different kinds of speech-acts used by both the mother and the child, we may better understand how interaction is shaped at each developmental point. This will mean examining how specific speech-acts are used by both mother and child to control, direct and maintain conversation.

Analysis of conversational exchanges

The philosophical analysis of conversations makes clear what conversationalists necessarily do and are capable of. According to Grice's (1975) and Bach and Harnish's (1979) accounts, the various meanings which are implicated by the speaker and inferred by the hearer in conversational discourse follow from general principles which govern all aspects of human interaction. Speaker and hearer follow a chain of inferences from the literal meaning to the meaning in context on the basis of reasonable assumptions about the world and people's interactions in it. As in the case of speech-act theory, philosophical inquiry presumes communicative competence, a presumption which cannot be made when discussing children's conversational behavior. Consequently, it is necessary for students of children's language to first explore in detail what children have to acquire in order to become mature, competent conversationalists. The child's capacity to recognize and adhere to the universal rules defined by Grice will necessarily reflect the intellectual grasp of various assumptions about the world which emerges at each stage in his or her development. The relationship between the child's growing conversational ability and the quality of his social knowledge must therefore be clearly understood. This again requires an integration of the efforts of both students of child language and those of social development.

The aim, then, of empirical research becomes that of charting the developing child's ability to use conversational rules both to guide his or her own language use and to process the correct meaning of the linguistic utterance in question, at each development stage. A subsidiary concern is that of examining how children acquire and develop not only the literal meaning of an utterance, but also its conversationally implied or conveyed meaning.

A note on the prelinguistic bases of children's language

The focus of this book is on the nature and development of children's language and their ability to participate in conversation. This said it is important to note that the origins of conversation can be traced to early infancy and prelinguistic behavior. Thus as a precursor to the discussion of child language and social development presented in chapter 3, I conclude with a brief review of the research on the prelinguistic foundations of communicative competence.

Research indicates that the infant acquires a whole mass of behaviors on which later conversational ability depends in a gradual way. It has often been assumed that newborns lack any basic social skills and that their requirements are purely physiological. A number of recent studies on the neonate's behavior tend to refute this view. In fact, it is now apparent that infants are biologically predisposed for communication from the moment of birth. Moments after birth, infants display an interest in the human face which is prior to any interest in objects (Fantz, 1965). Their crying is another example of neonates' behavior which carries clear social connotations. Gaze behavior taking place between infant and adult is identical to that found in adult verbal conversations (Jaffe and Feldstein, 1970), and mutual gaze is present from three months onwards.

While such research does indicate a clear predisposition to sociality, it is important to distinguish such early behaviors from later ones which are used with a clear intention to communicate. As Sugarman-Bell (1978) points out, communication involves more than the emitting of a behavior with a high social potency. Rather, it involves the *intention* to convey an idea to someone else. This distinguishes communication from the production of mere expressive or other interpretable behaviors. Hence the main question becomes: How do babies develop the ability to use these behaviors intentionally?

Most researchers have pointed out that communicative behavior develops as a result of the child's social experiences, in particular his or her interactions with the care-taker (e.g. Keenan, 1974; Snow, 1977; McTear, 1985; Sugarman-Bell, 1978). Perhaps the most obvious point is that adults treat and behave towards their children *as if* they have clear intentions and *as if* they are full participants in a conversation, while in fact the children are only gradually becoming so. Research demonstrates that care-takers respond selectively to their infant's gestures and vocalizations, focusing on those which are meaningful in adult communication. Later on, care-takers create and maintain the discourse structure for their children, teaching them in a sense how to participate in that structure and eventually appropriate it. But, most importantly, care-takers respond to some of the child's actions as if they were communicative (E. V. Clark, 1978). Thus human babies become human beings because they are treated *as if* they are already human beings. A similar line of argument is advanced by Bruner (1975) in his analysis of the possible importance of mother–infant interaction for language development. He claims that one of the earliest principles of communication to be acquired is that particular behaviors receive predictable responses. Examining games like "give and take" and "peekaboo," Bruner shows how such games help the child learn to make correct responses to the care-taker's elicitations, or take turns, anticipate actions and eventually initiate episodes.

By the time the infant is 9 or 10 months old, it becomes possible to attribute to the infant's behaviors the intention to communicate meanings. Around the 10th month the first clearly intentional acts, ones of requesting and of stating, are evident. The child begins to understand the role of adults as agents and the role of his or her own signals in affecting that agency. Thus the child can use an object to attract his or her mother's attention (a proto-declarative) or the gesture of "pointing" to make a proto-imperative. The following is an example of an imperative sequence from a 12-month-old child:

> C. is seated in a corridor in front of the kitchen door. She looks towards her mother and calls with an acute sound "ha." M. comes over to her, and C. looks towards the kitchen twisting her body and upper shoulders to do so. M. carries her into the kitchen and C. points towards the sink. M. gives her a glass of water, and C. drinks it eagerly.

> (Bates *et al.*, 1979, p. 121)

By the 15th month the act of requesting becomes more sophisticated. The child has specific vocalizations which accompany different non-verbal behaviors (Bruner, 1981). At the same time, mothers' expectations towards their children increase. They expect them not only to take a turn but also to provide appropriate responses (Snow, 1977). By the age of 2 the child can use language, and some elements of conversational ability are evident. The child is able to maintain continuity (Keenan, 1974) and to respond to most questions addressed to him or her appropriately (de Villiers and de Villiers, 1979). However, the communication ability of the 2-year-old child is severely limited. He or she is egocentric in the use of language and has major problems in placing speech in the right context and comprehending speech which is not relevant to the topic at hand. This brings us to issues of child language proper, which are explored in the following chapter.

3 Language use and social functioning

The general aim of the present book is to discover what children can and cannot do with language at different periods in their development. As suggested by the analysis of language presented in chapters 1 and 2, two parameters of language use are of particular interest: (a) the development of speech-acts, and (b) the development of conversational competence and the understanding of "conversational meaning." My review of the philosophical literature on adult linguistic communication suggests the following points of orientation for the analysis of children's language use:

(a) Speech-acts:
  (i) Speech-acts are well differentiated and serve many purposes.
  (ii) A highly developed ability is needed to maintain and control interaction and conversation with the use of specific speech-acts (e.g. with the use of requestives).

(b) Conversational competence and conversational meaning
  (i) An understanding of intentional communication.
  (ii) An understanding of the social context of an utterance.
  (iii) An understanding that for the successful comprehension of some utterances the hearer needs to make certain inferences.
  (iv) An understanding that speech contributions must be relevant to the discourse at hand and must be coordinated with the listener's perspective.

My own research focuses on the development of both speech-acts and conversational competence. In both cases, the aim is to offer an analysis of the abilities children evidence at different developmental periods. This entails the following:

(a) *Speech-acts.* Investigating both the kinds of social functions language performs in a social context at different developmental periods and the ways in which speech-acts expand to serve a more complex and more sophisticated interaction. Furthermore, given that speech-acts are embedded in social situations and contribute to the shaping of interaction that individuals participate in, there is also an interest in investigating the nature of the interaction that children are able to engage in at different developmental periods.

(b) *Conversational competence.* Examining the interpretative process that occurs in conversational exchanges. Here the interest is in a developmental analysis of linguistic communication and the inferential abilities which help young children to see conversational acts as accomplishments of social episodes. This will require an examination of the degree to which the child is able to cooperate with his or her conversational partner and infer communicative intentions. The main belief of the present work is that this understanding is more social than linguistic because it depends on the child's developing ability to take the perspective of others and of the social situation into account. To understand how such an ability develops, both language and social functioning in general will be examined. The analysis here will focus on one particular speech-act – the act of asserting. How assertions are performed and to what extent the child's assertive responses are relevant to ongoing conversation will be examined. At the same time, the analysis will concentrate on examining what kind of assertions are performed and how successful they are.

The present chapter lays the foundation for this inquiry. It begins with a review of the research on children's language development. The focus here is on that small body of work which examines children's speech-acts. Following this, the work on communicative competence is then discussed. Again the amount of work done is limited, but important insights are offered. A particular concern addressed is that of the child's growing ability to understand indirect and non-literal utterances. This consideration of children's language use leads directly to a consideration of their social development, particularly their socio-cognitive development. Throughout, an attempt is made both to draw on the insights offered by these several lines of research and to clarify what work remains to be done.

The development of children's language: a review of the research

The review presented here sketches the development of children's language from its emergence in infancy through to late childhood. Consistent with the analysis of language in chapter 2, the focus is on research which examines children's speech-acts and their conversational competence. The aim of this review is both to discuss what is known and to identify important areas of inquiry which have been neglected.

Speech-acts

The performance of speech-acts depends on the child's ability to use words with intent. As noted in the previous chapter, the intention to communicate meanings can be attributed to the child's behavior around the 9th or 10th month. At this time, the first isolated words appear (Dale, 1972). In most cases, these are two-syllable approximations of adult words. This is also the time when a comprehension of highly specified speech discriminations of word pairs (e.g. "bet", "pet") begins to emerge (Nelson, 1973). At about the 12th month, one-word utterances appear. Usually these are meaningful expressions of person and object names and some relational words (e.g. "up," "no," "more"). There is also evidence of a nascent comprehension of simple instructions and questions, and of first participation in simple conversations and naming games. Around the 18th month, mothers start correcting their children's speech both in terms of content and pronunciation (Snow, 1977). Most of the questions addressed to children of this age simply require yes–no answers. Children quite ably discriminate such questions from *wh-* questions and respond appropriately (Rodgon, 1979). By the age of 2, the child is able to combine words to express semantic relations (e.g. agent, action).

At the time when his or her language abilities are first emerging, the child is very tied to the immediate environment. The sentences he or she uses are very simple and involve objects and events that take place within the "here and now" of personal experience. Most of his or her assertions are labelings of events or objects. At this early stage, the child's speech seems to be mainly of a responsive type. This is not surprising given that the literature suggests that adults' speech to young children has been consistently found to contain a high proportion of questions (Snow, 1977; McShane, 1980). As illustrated in the work of Sacks *et al.* (1974), questions provide a powerful means of regulating turn allocation. Thus the prevalence of questions can be viewed as part of the care-taker's attempt to construct a conversational interaction with the child. By the age of $2\frac{1}{2}$, children's language contains fewer instances of labeling. With an increase of vocabulary, the child's assertions become far more complex than simply labels of objects. At the end of the 2nd year, a "doggie" becomes "doggie on table" or "I like doggie" (McShane, 1980). By the age of 3, the child begins to further exploit the semantic potential of language to refer beyond the "here and now." By that age, Ervin-Tripp (1977a) found instances in children's language of recall of events, whether prompted or not, which made reference to potential events.

Another main category of speech-acts found in child language at an early age is that of requests. In particular, the development of requests for action can be traced back to the early prelinguistic stage. From about the age of 9 months, children's gestures and vocalizations can be interpreted with some reliability as intentional requesting schemas. Based on a detailed and careful observation of one child between 12 and 16 months, Carter (1978) describes a range of different communicative schemata, including requests. One of the most common was the request for action. This was realized by an open-handed gesture towards an object along with a vocalization of an /m/ initial monosyllable. Similarly, Halliday (1975) reports the use of vocalizations such as /na/ at age 0;9–0;10 and /mnn/ at age 1;1–1;3, which he interpreted respectively as "I want this" and "Give me that." Ervin-Tripp (1977b) reviews a number of accounts of the early use and development of verbal requests. Early in the 2nd year, the first requests are realized by combinations of gestures with names of desired objects and words such as "more," and "want." By the age of $2\frac{1}{2}$, children start using conventional request forms, like "Can I" and "Can you."

By the time they are 3, children's language ability expands enormously. Their assertions become more differentiated and complex. As a result, they are able to engage in pretend play which is verbally defined and to participate in more extended conversational episodes. Similar developments occur in the child's responsives. As language matures, replies are minimized in length, being focused on the crucial element in question. At this age, children could usually give categorically appropriate replies to *what* questions and could answer with animate objects to *who* questions (Ervin-Tripp, 1970). However, all children had difficulty with *how*, *when*, *where from* and *why* questions. Indeed, most children require a full year to comprehend the above forms of *wh-* questions. Children's requestives are also developing. The children progress from the primitive "gimme" of the previous stage to more subtle and diverse requesting which is more characteristic of adult speech. As Ervin-Tripp (1978a) reports, it is after the third year that one can see socially biased requests, embedded imperatives (e.g. "Would you") and polite markers (e.g. "Please," "Could you") accompanying direct requests.

Two points need to be made about this research. First, little work has been done which examines a given speech-act across a span of years. Thus there is insufficient information on the development of speech-acts. Second, no research has been conducted which examines speech-acts other than those mentioned. Consequently, nothing is known of the child's use of expressives, commissives or acknowledgments – speech-acts which are critical to the effective use of language and the regulation of conversation. One purpose of my own work (reported in chapters 4, 5 and 6) is to fill these gaps, that is to provide a detailed descriptive model of speech-acts.

Conversational competence

Apart from the need to learn more differentiated and complex speech-acts, the child must learn to become a better conversationalist. He or she must learn to adapt his or her speech to the listener's needs, to produce relevant discourse and to construct coherent sequences of dialogue. In addition, the child must learn how to get attention, initiate conversation, and discern when the standing questions have been answered or the topic has been resolved. As Ervin-Tripp (1979) points out, a 2-year-old cannot do the above, so that "jumping" properly into adult conversation, for example, is a very difficult task. Ervin-Tripp and Gordon's (1980) analysis of videotapes of four families photographed in natural settings indicates that when other people were talking, the 2-year-olds just blurted out requests 89% of the time. In comparison, only 31% of the school-age youngsters did that. The older children interrupted conversations by using polite markers or excuses. Moreover, they not only tried to get attention more often, but in so doing used more effective attention-getters (e.g. calling out "Hey Joe," instead of just "Hey").

As already mentioned, an important ability that the child has to develop is the construction of coherent discourse. Participants in conversation rely on certain cohesive devices such as anaphoric reference (e.g. he, she) or discourse connectors (e.g. as a matter of fact, actually) to illustrate the relevance of one sentence to another. However, as McTear (1985) rightly points out, participants rely on more than surface markers of cohesion in their construction of relevant discourse. Utterances are related to each other. Usually the first utterance sets up certain expectations as to what utterance will follow. Thus a request for action predicts a response related to the request which can be either compliant or non-compliant. Responses are therefore inspected for their relevance in the light of the discourse expectations set by preceding initiations.

How then does the child develop the ability to understand one utterance as being related to another and to produce coherent discourse? At the beginning of language development, the child is too immature to keep track of coherence. His or her language is tied to the immediate environment and it is usually the adult who provides the links from one utterance to another. By age 2, we see one of the first instances of the child's attempt to recognize expectations concerning the type of utterance which follows a question. At this age, the child replies to questions even when he or she does not understand what precisely is being asked. He or she thereby evidences an awareness of the expectation that a request must be followed by a response (Ervin-Tripp, 1979; McShane, 1980).

One of the earliest cohesive devices used by young children involves repetition of all or part of the preceding utterance. Development from such immature to more adult-like conversational strategies has been investigated by Keenan (1974) and Keenan and Klein (1975). They report that the strategy of repetition was used at age 2;9 as a means of responding to adults' questions. By age 3, however, this had given way to the strategy of substitution. McTear (1985, p. 62) quotes the following example:

A: flower broken, flower
B: many flowers broken

Here we see speaker B repeating part of the utterances, thus achieving cohesion, but substituting a word and thereby adding information.

At the same time, by age 3, the children investigated by Keenan also started using anaphoric pronouns instead of repeating preceding utterances. Ervin-Tripp (1978a) reports the following developments in children between the ages of 2;9 and 3;6: (1) the appearance of auxiliary ellipses in responses, for example "Mary was," "I did it"; (2) the use of pronouns in replies to refer back to previously mentioned nouns; and (3) the use of conjunctions to connect sentences across turns. In the last case development reflects the cognitive difficulty of the relationships indicated. Addition is the first to be expressed (e.g. *and, also*). This is followed by connectives denoting temporal change (e.g. *then*), adversative contrast (e.g. *but, though*) and finally condition. McTear (1985) found the use of *because* present in his daughter's speech at around age 3. Between the ages of $3\frac{1}{2}$ and 4, both the children McTear investigated started using *well, sure, anyway* and *otherwise* as cohesive devices. However, the children did not use any discourse connectors judged to be more mature ones, like *mind you*, *frankly*, *actually* or *as a matter of fact*. McTear's speculation is that these devices develop later on and are representative of children's language at school age.

The child's ability to link utterances and produce relevant discourse marks another major development in his or her language, the development of a more open conversational structure. The path here is from the tendency to use more closed exchanges consisting of initiation and response sequences to the tendency to use more open exchange structures – where exchanges are linked by utterances with the dual function of responding to a preceding utterance and initiating a further response (McTear, 1985).

The evidence presented thus far suggests that the 3-year-old is quite competent in his or her language usage. By that age, the child already has a good vocabulary and can communicate successfully with people in the immediate environment. He or she is already able to use language to initiate conversations (Ervin-Tripp, 1977a; Keenan, 1974) and is increasingly able to control the information received by querying or by using tag constructions (Garvey, 1977; Berlinger and Garvey, 1981). As a conversational partner, however, he or she is still severely limited. The conversational exchanges he or she is engaging in are necessarily short and the cohesive devices used are not elaborated. Furthermore, the child often fails to take the perspective of another person adequately into account and to adapt his or her language accordingly (de Villiers and de Villiers, 1979). It is after the 3rd year that we can observe the beginnings of such developments.

The ability to take the perspective of the other person into account and tailor one's behavior accordingly is crucial to cooperative exchange and conversation. With regard to the study of children's language, the issue here is one of their linguistic egocentrism. This has been investigated through studies of referential communication. Most of these have been influenced by Piaget's (1959) theory of egocentrism. Piaget (1959) himself has concluded that the preschool child is egocentric in nature and unable to develop representations about people in social situations. Because he or she cannot take into account the listener's perspective when structuring the content of messages, his or her early communication is necessarily deficient. However, many later studies conflict with this position. Most of these have studied children's conversations in naturalistic settings and found that children are able to take the perspective of another person into account much earlier than believed by Piagetians. For example, Shatz and Gelman (1973) tested children aged $4\frac{1}{2}$ and found an ability to adjust their speech to the listener's demands. The $4\frac{1}{2}$-year-olds treated 2-year-olds quite differently from adults. Speech directed to the 2-year-olds was devoid of any statements about mental states and any requests about complex information. The children's main goal was to get the 2-year-olds' attention, to which end they employed speech which was of a repetitive kind, containing many attention-getters and *what* questions.

When considering the question of linguistic egocentrism, it is important to remember that it is not an all-or-nothing matter. The development of successful communication is a gradual process. As we saw, at $4\frac{1}{2}$ years, we have the first conscious attempts to adjust the speech to the social context. Yet children at this age still have problems. Spilton and Lee (1977) studied the speech adaptations of 5-year-olds to a peer listener's adaptations during free play. The authors found that the language used seemed very adaptive, but also that most questions occurring during the peer interaction were of a highly general nature. As Spilton and Lee argued, the high frequency of general questions (which are not very predictive of an adaptive response) suggests that 5-year-olds might not be very competent as listeners and might adopt that strategy in order to minimize the chances of unsuccessful communication. Of course, it may equally be the case that this strategy is the only strategy available in the 5-year-old's language repertoire. Peterson *et al.* (1972) studied the developmental changes in children's responses to three indications of communicative failure. Both 4- and 7-year-old children readily reformulated their initial messages when explicitly requested to do so by the listener. In contrast, only the 7-year-olds tended to reformulate their messages in response to an implicit rather than an explicit verbal request for additional help (such as "I don't understand"). There was evidence that the 4-year-olds did interpret the latter type of feedback as a request for help, but did not understand what kind of help was needed. Finally, children of both age groups failed to reformulate their message when confronted only with non-verbal, facial expressions of the listener's non-comprehension.

The research on the development of children's conversational abilities has yielded valuable insights into the gradual process whereby these abilities develop. However, no attempt has been made to investigate and compare all the maxims of good conversational participation as they emerge in the course of a child's development. Instead, there are a small number of separate studies each of which focuses on a limited number of conversational parameters and does so with regard to children of a limited age range. In the research I report in the following chapters, I attempt a more comprehensive exploration of children's conversation and examine a longer segment of a child's development.

Conversational meaning: the case of indirect and non-literal utterances

To become fully competent conversationalists, children must eventually develop the ability to go beyond the consideration of the form of an utterance to a consideration of its function. In so doing, they must recognize that a particular utterance can perform many different functions. Depending on the circumstances, children have to develop the ability to interpret an utterance in constative form, not only as a constative but also as a complaint, a question, an accusation, an attribution of negative qualities, or possibly an invitation to contradiction. As argued in chapter 2, in order to understand the communicative intent of an utterance, the hearer must be able to make certain kinds of inferences concerning the other person's intentions and the appropriateness of the context of the current discourse via the contextual parameters. Although much research has been done on children's language abilities, little is known of the ways in which children develop a concept of communicative intent and thus come to understand not only what is said but also what is implied. To be able to interpret the speaker's communicative intentions the hearer must have (1) an understanding of the direction of discourse and of the mutual knowledge which underlies the context of discourse; (2) an understanding of the fact that the speaker performs a particular utterance with a given intention in mind; and (3) an understanding that some situations are in need of an inference if communication is to be successful.

Let's examine in detail what the child must know in order to perform and understand the act of asserting successfully. The first condition is the "preparatory" condition (Searle, 1969). This condition states that the device X is to be used only if the hearer is or might be in a position to understand the desired effect and the speaker believes that the hearer is in such a position. Translating the above condition in terms of the performance of assertions, the child needs (1) a specific linguistic knowledge consisting of understanding the conventional form of behavior involved in giving something a name and treating that word thereafter as the thing's name (the linguistic assumption); and (2) an understanding that asserting is a cooperative activity which is based on certain pragmatic presuppositions. In particular, if the speaker is using the sentence appropriately in a given context, he must pragmatically presuppose that (a) the hearer is able to perceive X or the state of affairs, (b) the hearer must know that X is the name of something, and (c) the hearer must currently either attend to X or can arrive at X via the common ground of the discourse.

For producing and understanding literal or direct assertions, the above conditions are not problematic for young children. It has already been argued that $2\frac{1}{2}$–3-year-olds operate in accordance with those conditions and are able to both direct attention and refer to something in the external world. The capacity to acquire and direct adult attention develops during the non-verbal period (Atkinson and Griffith, 1973). Ervin-Tripp analyzed the conversational exchanges of $2\frac{1}{2}$-year-olds and gave examples of children's assertions. In asserting "A battery, this is a battery. Look battery. Battery is Jiji's," the child aims at making a reference about something in the external world, claiming that a particular object belongs to someone else. By uttering "look," the child verbally attempts both to ensure that the hearer attends to the referred object and to establish that object as part of their common ground. In this particular example, the conversation continues with the hearer, who states: "Get one, I'll play with that one." Here, the hearer continues the conversation and uses the word "one" to signal to the speaker that he is in fact attending to the aforementioned object. From then on, the object is treated as a part of their common ground.

In the case of indirect or non-literal assertions, however, the situation becomes far more complex. To recognize the presence of indirect or non-literal expressions, the child must not only make inferences concerning the other person's inner state, but also inferences about what the present discourse context involves and what is appropriate or inappropriate. Moreover, he or she needs to infer that, under the particular circumstances, either the speaker could not *merely* be implying X (and thus the speaker is producing an indirect act) or that there is a certain recognizable relation in saying P and implying R (e.g. in metaphorical language). The child faced with such utterances has first to infer the literal or direct meaning of the utterance and then conclude that this reading is inappropriate in the present context. To understand the intended meaning, the child must search via the maxim of relevance for an interpretation which makes the utterance relevant to the particular topic or issue at hand.

Virtually all the developmental research on conversational analysis deals only with one limited aspect of pragmatics, namely forms of requests and their responses. Ervin-Tripp (1977b) hypothesized that children's use of forms of requests progresses from direct imperatives (e.g. "Gimme cookies") to indirect requests based on conversational postulates (e.g. "Those look nice"). Although children seem to be better at comprehending than at producing indirect requests, recent empirical studies on the use of request forms have generally confirmed this prediction. Shatz (1975) examined 2-year-olds' responses to direct and indirect requests from their mothers. She found no difference in the likelihood of compliance to direct versus indirect requests. It may be that the young children in this study did interpret indirect requests correctly on the basis of the context in which they were uttered. But it is equally possible that they were relying on non-verbal cues from the mother or only on parts of the request (e.g. interpreting an utterance like "Can you shut the door" as "Shut the door"). Focusing on the production of requests, Bates (1976) examined 2–4-year-olds interacting with their mothers. She found that virtually all such requests by children were either conventional commands, "Can I have" requests, or statements of desire (e.g. "I want that"). Indirect requests based on conversational postulates do not usually appear until ages $3\frac{1}{2}$–4 at least.

A number of researchers have presented evidence that 2- and 3-year-old children often respond to indirect commands or assertions as if they were direct ones (e.g. Ervin-Tripp, 1978a; Shatz, 1978). This work also suggests they have great difficulty in understanding and producing metaphorical or sarcastic language. The analytical problems here are, however, more complex than they initially appear. As Ervin-Tripp (1981) and Ervin-Tripp and Gordon (1980) have argued, it is important to distinguish between the traditional direct–indirect dichotomy (which relies on surface syntax) and the dichotomy of explicit–implicit requests. For example, embedded directives (which usually fall in the category of indirect speech) are extremely explicit and thus are acquired early in life. Moreover, children as young as 2 years can respond appropriately to requests in the form "Can you . . .?" and even to requests in which the desired act is not stated, as in "Are there any more cookies?" (Shatz, 1975). However, they also respond with actions to utterances which do not necessarily require an action. Thus Shatz has argued that children operate with an action-based rule of the form "mother says – child does." In her (1975) discrimination experiment, children were presented with utterances containing "Can you" + feasible act in two discourse contexts, one following a series of directives and one following an information exchange. It was found that even in the information exchange context, children showed a bias towards action-based responses. It is therefore argued that older children develop away from this action-based strategy by learning the appropriate linguistic and contextual markers for various illocutionary acts.

The most comprehensive work so far on the children's understanding of requests was carried through by Ervin-Tripp and her colleagues (Ervin-Tripp, 1981; Ervin-Tripp and Gordon, 1980). They examined children's responses to direct and indirect requests in two types of situations. In the first, a helping situation, a problem was created in which the speaker in the story could be heard as asking for help. For example, a mother walks up to the front door carrying bags of groceries and discovers the door closed. The mother says to the child "Is the door open?" or "The door is closed." In the second situation, the prohibiting situation, a naughty act was depicted (e.g. children painting on the living-room wall) and the speaker could be heard asking the children to stop. The results of the study indicated that the situation itself played an important role in whether the child understands explicit or implicit requests. In the helping situation, 92% of all subjects responded appropriately to the most explicit and conventional requests (e.g. "Can you . . .?"). As the requests became increasingly implicit, the 3-year-olds became less and less cooperative. The 9-year-olds were more cooperative in helping. In contrast, the prohibiting situation produced quite different behaviour. All children, regardless of age, responded appropriately. This finding suggests that the situation and the children's background knowledge as to what is right or wrong helps them make sense of something that they are not yet cognitively or linguistically in a position to understand.

Question directives and implicit requests (hints) are less explicit than embedded directives and in most cases they do not mention the desired goal, state or object at all. Consequently, their comprehension depends either on repeated conjunction with more explicit forms or on certain contextual cues which have become conventionalized in the child's life or on active inference by the hearer. Ervin-Tripp (1979) argues that, from age 4 on, the comprehension of complex indirect speech-acts increases. However, in his study of 4-year-olds, McTear (1985) did not find a developmental trend away from direct imperatives to more indirect forms. As he suggests, this can be explained in terms of the particular context of the requests. Given that most of the requests were directed to a peer in play, one can expect direct imperatives to predominate. McTear found that both his children used some hints in requesting and that some of these hints displayed evidence of strategic ploys on the part of the speaker. Analyzing the request strategy used by the children at different developmental periods, McTear found that complex conditions such as reference to the possible consequences of a request act develop late (around age 5), whereas querying the need for the request or the action using a simple *why* question occurs earlier. Moreover, denial of obligation occurs early, whereas denial of willingness occurs late.

The development in the child's use and understanding of indirection may require considerable knowledge of the practical, social and technical facts needed to make a successful inference. Thus, as Ervin-Tripp (1979) rightly points out, we can expect variation across children in the rate of development because of social and environmental factors which affect their access to these relevant facts. Although there is environmentally created variation among children, broad differences between all children and adults remain. Although by the 4th or 5th year children are able to use diverse syntactic forms, they still refer explicitly to their desires and goals when these are not obvious from the context. So the major difference between adults and children, as Ervin-Tripp concludes, "is not diversity of structure nor diversity of social features – though the rules may increase in number of variables and in complexity with age – but [the use by children of] systematic, regular unmarked utterances" (Ervin-Tripp, 1979, p. 188) which either do not refer to what the speaker wants or which do not show an ability to use the intentions of speakers in developing elaborated strategies as a means to a communicative goal.

This research represents an important pioneering effort in the analysis of indirectness in children's conversation. In my own research, I attempt to take this work a step further. This is done in two ways. First, greater attention is paid to conceptual issues in the analysis of indirection. In particular, an attempt is made to distinguish various forms of indirect speech and the particular requirements associated with the understanding of each of them. Second, and following on the first, a detailed analysis is offered of the naturally occurring conversations of a large number of children from ages $3\frac{1}{2}$ to 7.

As this brief review suggests, the little research that has been done on the development of the child's understanding of conversational meaning has focused on indirection. None has directly studied the development of the child's understanding of non-literality in the child's everyday conversations. There have been a number of experimental studies examining children's comprehension of metaphoric utterances (Gardner *et al.*, 1978; Winner *et al.*, 1980; Vosniadou *et al.*, 1984) and a few experiments studying the children's understanding of idioms (Prinz, 1983; Gibbs, 1987). Generally, these studies have reported an increase in children's comprehension of metaphors or idioms. When children have to either explain verbally or choose the appropriate pictorial meaning of metaphors or idioms, such as "Don't go out on a limb," they tend to give literal interpretations. It is only later on, around the ages of 8 or 9, that children start viewing metaphoric or idiomatic expressions as having figurative meanings. However, what do we know of the child's ability to comprehend and produce non-literal utterances during his or her natural conversational interactions? The research reported in chapters 4, 5 and 6 provides some initial evidence on this matter. The analysis of adult conversation suggests that for the hearer to understand non-literal expressions (be they direct or indirect), he or she must be aware of specific conventional agreements (rules) which are culturally used to refer to things (e.g. metaphors) and which facilitate action interpretation in social exchanges. Turning to children's conversation, it is clear that the child must be able to take the perspective of others into account and to view speech-acts addressed to him or her as intentional. He or she must also have a considerable knowledge of the social facts needed to arrive at the intentional goal. The research presented in the following chapters suggests that children are able to cope with non-literality after their 6th year. It is my belief that this ability continues to develop until adolescence, when the function of social rules is fully recognized.

In the preceding pages, I have reviewed a variety of studies which combine to provide an initial glimpse of the development of children's language ability. All of these developments – those in speech-acts, in conversational behavior and in conversational meaning – are of crucial importance to the child's becoming a successful and cooperative communicator. A key claim I wish to make here is that this entire spectrum of developments depends primarily on the growth of the child's understanding of the needs of others and his or her willingness to gratify them. The key assumption – and one that is central to my research – is that because development here depends on the child's growing ability to take the perspective of others into account, it must be considered to be more social than linguistic.

The development of the child's conversational ability in light of his or her social understanding

Thus far discussion has centered on one aspect of the development of the ability to become a good conversational partner. The emphasis has been on examining how the child understands not only what is grammatically said, but also what is conversationally meant (i.e. whether a particular act is an act of referring, predicating, promising, etc.). As argued earlier, this focus on language in use and on conversational behavior necessarily leads to a consideration of social interactions and the knowledge they presuppose. Social interaction, in the abstract sense intended here, can be understood as a sustained production of chains of mutually dependent acts constructed by two or more agents, each monitoring and building on the actions of the other. In analyzing social interaction, an attempt must be made to determine what necessary and jointly sufficient conditions must be met in order for that highly coordinated kind of interdependent behavior to take place. Armed with a knowledge of these conditions, we are better able to study children's language use, an activity which has the development of social understanding at its core.

Most pragmatists working in the area of child language assume an interdependence of language and social functioning. For example, Ervin-Tripp (1981, p. 208) asserts that "interpersonal control acts always involve both information about social assumptions and relationships, and information about desired acts or goals." Similarly, McTear (1985, p. 202) suggests that "one only has to consider the inability of children to unravel the temporal and logical sequence of events in a film intended for adult viewers or to understand the humor in an adult comedy show, to recognize the extent to which competent participation in adult interaction depends on a degree of knowledge of the world which is beyond the experience of the young child."

Claims such as those quoted above are typical. Nonetheless, there are very few studies which attempt to examine in detail the interdependence of language and social functioning. Flavell (1968) gives an account of experimental work which links referential communication and role-taking ability in children. Karmiloff-Smith (1979) investigated the use of the definite and indefinite article and linked the appropriate usage of such articles to the overall cognitive ability of the child to assess the extent of the listener's knowledge. Both studies concluded that children's use of language becomes socially more appropriate with age owing to an increasing sensitivity to the listener's perspective and an increasing cognitive ability to assess the other's state of knowledge. However, there is no study in the literature which attempts to examine the development of conversational behavior together with the development of social functioning. My aims, therefore, are to specify the main parameters of social functioning which are related to competent language usage and to examine how this relation works in everyday conversations. As has been repeatedly argued, language understanding and communicative competence depend on the child's increasing understanding of the social perspective of others. When people perform various social acts by using language, choose among alternative ways of saying the same thing, determine when to say what they want according to the appropriate context, and engage in the highly cooperative activity we call conversation, they always do so by taking the perspective of the listener and adapting their language accordingly.

When studying language in the context of social cognition, I have isolated several important aspects of the child's socio-cognitive development which appear to be relevant to communicative competence in general. They include:

(1) The development of inferences about others and the ability to role-take. Here we include (a) the ability to understand that a particular situation is in need of an inference, (b) the ability to attribute to other people inner states (e.g. intentions, beliefs), (c) the understanding that other people's inner states may be different from yours, and (d) the understanding of "agency" and human action (i.e. means–ends relationships, consequent and antecedent acts, and goal-directed behavior).

(2) The understanding of social rules and social contexts. Here we include (a) children's reasoning about social rules and social contexts and (b) children's knowledge of the usual sequences of events and roles.

(3) Knowledge of certain linguistic conventions, that is knowledge of certain conventional uses of words (e.g. metaphors).

Although not much research has been done on the development of these abilities as they relate to language understanding, children's social development has been the subject of many studies. One focus of this effort has been children's ability to make inferences regarding inner psychological states. Following the Piagetian position, it was assumed that children had to be capable of concrete operational thinking before being able to make any kind of inferences about another person's inner state. The classical example of that position is the belief that children below the age of 7 or 8 typically make the egocentric error of attributing their own point of view to a doll. This position, however, has been challenged by researchers working from within the Piagetian framework. Bryant (1975) has found that if you change the classical Piagetian designs and make sure that memory controls are made, children as young as 4 can make certain kinds of inferences. To the same end, Shantz (1975) has argued that children do understand the perspective of the other person if the situation is more familiar and relevant to them than the classical "doll and mountain" experiment (see p. 44).

The criticisms of the Piagetian approach generated new research designs which aimed at investigating the social abilities of children as young as 3 years old. These new designs have marked a shift in the general conceptual framework guiding the study of social interaction. As Shantz (1975) argues, the research conducted until that point (i.e. that adopting a sociological or

Piagetian approach) had relied on an experimental design in its attempt to assess children's abilities in interactional contexts. In so doing, this research had failed to capture the dialectics of subject-to-subject interaction. Children's social knowledge is not acquired independently of their active participation in social interaction. Consequently, research must focus on interaction contexts and examine how they foster children's social development. Interactions present the child with occasional behaviors and circumstances which are discrepant with his or her expectations. This provides the child with continuous corrective feedback regarding the interpretations he or she makes of the other's behavior and inner states, and it motivates the child to attempt a reassessment. As this analysis suggests, we need to study not only the development of social knowledge, but also the social development of knowledge.

Social cognitive development as it relates to language usage

The development of inferences about others

One inference about others which has received considerable attention in recent years is that of inner psychological states. The evidence suggests that the ability to attribute inner states to other people develops quite early in life. As Keasy (1979) has shown, 3- and 4-year-old children ask *why* questions, suggesting that they are beginning to concentrate on the psychological motives of others. Borke (1971) found that in a familiar and highly motivated natural setting, 3-year-old children make few errors regarding other people's feelings. In her study of the representation of emotion, Shields (1985) demonstrated that 3-year-old children operate with an implicit two-phase model (steady versus upset emotional states) which begins to be more differentiated at age 5. This claim receives support from Flavell (1974), who argues that a 4-year-old child shows some limited knowledge of some sort of inferences about others' emotional states, especially if these are simple (i.e. sadness versus happiness, or goodness versus badness).

Flavell (1968), however, asserts that a distinction should be made between the child's ability to understand intentions and his or her ability to understand motives. In fact, as Keasy (1979) argues, the concept of intentionality and the concept of motive seem to follow different developmental sequences. The concept of motive emerges earlier. Whereas the concept of motive deals with what a particular motive behind an act is (e.g. bad or good), the concept of intentionality deals with whether the action was accidental or motivated. As Keasy argues, children at the age of 3 already seem able to differentiate between good and bad motives, the concept of bad being learned before the concept of good. In contrast, it is not much before their 6th birthday that children seem able to differentiate clearly between accidental and intentional events and to attribute to people subjective responsibility for their actions. This claim is consistent with Fein's (1972) findings, which showed that although 4-year-olds were able to perceive the causality of social pictures this ability increased with age and accurate statements were achieved only after the age of 6.

It is reasonable to assume, then, that before the age of 5 children have a notion of a psychological force, but that this notion is global and undifferentiated. After the age of 5, children begin to make accurate distinctions between the possible causes of social phenomena and to understand the concept of intentionality. They consequently become increasingly able to differentiate between inner-subjective states and concrete behaviors and to understand the correct motives, thoughts and intentions which underlie overt behavior.

A second focus of research has been on the development of role-taking abilities. This work can be divided into two main paradigms. The first is Piaget and Inhelder's (1956) paradigm of visual-perspective-taking. The second is set by Flavell (1968), who investigated situations which depend upon the child recognizing and accommodating to the thoughts, feelings and intentions (as well as the precepts) of another person.

Piaget and Inhelder (1956) report a number of studies of the coordination of visual perspectives. One of them, the "doll and mountain" experiment, has virtually come to be regarded as the operational definition of spatial egocentrism. In this experiment, the child is presented with a three-dimensional model of three mountains. He or she is then asked to identify the visual perspective of a doll which was placed in several different positions from those of the child. Piaget and Inhelder (1956) distinguish three stages in the development of the children's performance in the experiment. In the first (between approximately 4 and 7 years), the children respond egocentrically. They tend to attribute their own perspective to the doll. Children aged 7 and 8 are in a transitional stage, where errors are made, but are not predominantly egocentric. However, it is not until 9 or 10 years of age that children perform without errors. In the first stage, it seems that children lack the knowledge that the appearance of objects is a function of the spatial position from which they are viewed. In the second, they have this knowledge, but only in the third stage do they acquire the ability to determine what that appearance would be for any specific viewing position.

It has already been noted that the classical Piagetian framework for studying role-taking abilities has been criticized as being inappropriate for young children. Later literature suggests that the ability to coordinate visual perspectives is a function of the particular task presented and that, in some circumstances, non-egocentric responses may already be elicited in 3- or 4-year-olds. Shantz and Watson (1971) used a task similar to that of the "doll and mountain," along with another in which the child himself moved and had to predict the view from his or her new position, the object being covered during the move. With $3\frac{1}{2}$- and $6\frac{1}{2}$-year-old children, the former task proved very difficult, yet the latter unexpectedly easy. Shantz and Watson (1971) suggest that in the former task the visible presence of the object seen by the child may make it harder to detach himself or herself from it in order to appreciate the other's point of view. They found that if the easier task was done first, it facilitated performance on the "doll and mountain" type of task. Huttenlocher and Presson (1973) obtained similar results on a task in which the child moved and had to predict his or her new view. Nigl and Fishbein (1974) raise an interesting point in relation to the Piagetian tasks. They argue that one should distinguish between social and conceptual aspects of perspective-taking tasks. Whereas conceptual aspects concern the inferences involved in the construction of the other's view, social aspects concern the child's tendency to select his or her own point of view, acting as though the instruction made reference to the child rather than to another person or the listener. Given such a distinction, our main concern is primarily with the social aspects of these tasks rather than with the conceptual one.

Moving even further down the age scale, a group of studies by Masangkay *et al.* (1974) demonstrated that children as young as $2\frac{1}{2}$ years old have the capacity for some basic inferences about visual perspective. For example, the child at this age can understand that when a card with a different picture on each side is interposed between the child and another person, that person can see the picture which the child cannot see. Thus it is safe to argue that from an early age the child appears to show some sensitivity to alternative visual perspectives. However, as Light (1979) points out, such sensitivity will probably only be manifest in very simple situations where the instructions are explicit.

Flavell (1968) conducted a wide-ranging study of role-taking in middle childhood and adolescence, providing valuable descriptions of the nature and pattern of acquisition of various abilities subsumed under the heading of role-taking. He divided the tasks used into two types: those involving a straightforward inference which might be correct or incorrect, and those in which there is no "right answer," but where the interest is in the degree of subtlety of the child's role-taking in the situation. The latter category involved all social guessing games which contained the potential infinite chain of inference, "I think that he is thinking that I am thinking . . . ." Most of the tasks Flavell used fell into the category in which there was not a "right" answer. For example, he used a picture story composed of seven pictures. When the child had "told" the story depicted, three of the pictures were removed and he or she was asked to say the story once again to another child who had not seen the original seven pictures. The sequence was so constructed that the remaining four pictures still made a meaningful story, but one which was significantly different from the original. The youngest children, 7-year-olds, grasped the original seven-picture story and could express it easily. But when presented with the four pictures, they told stories which evidenced various degrees of contamination from the original story.

Flavell (1968) also investigated communication aspects of role-taking. He argued that effective communication depends upon the child taking an accurate measure of the listener's role attributes and then actively using this knowledge to shape and adapt his messages accordingly. In one task, the child was asked to give instructions to another who was blindfolded in order to see whether the first child adapted the content of his or her messages accordingly. In another task, the child had to tell a story to a pictured 4-year-old child and then to a pictured adult. Flavell remarks that the 7-year-old children showed remarkable competence.

In all the research on children's performance of social cognitive tasks, a key problem faced by any researcher when a child fails on a task is to decide why the child fails. It is often difficult to determine whether the child does not know that others have different viewpoints (what Flavell has called the "existence" element), whether he or she is unaware that this is a task which requires this particular kind of knowledge (the "need" element), or whether he or she is simply having difficulty in working out the other's perspective (the "application" element). As Flavell (1968) has pointed out, it might even be wrong to conclude that the child considers his or her message to be adequate to a listener who cannot see. It is possible that the child fails to pay attention to this listener and thus fails to see the *need* to adapt his or her messages to the listener's needs. An apparent disparity between underlying abilities and actual performance has been noted in other studies. Levine and Hoffman (1975), in their study of empathy in 4-year-olds, point to a marked gap between the availability of inferential skills and the use made of them. Acredolo (1977) suggests that the period around 4 years of age may be one in which the gap between the ability to coordinate perspectives and the spontaneous use of such ability is particularly wide. She makes this suggestion on the basis of a study in which prompts and reminders were found to be uniquely effective in improving performance at this age.

The general conclusion to be drawn from the research is that some basic forms of role-taking emerge very early in childhood. These are, however, initially fragile, situation-specific and heavily dependent upon contextual and instructional cues. Thus preschool children are capable of cooperative behaviors (Garvey and Hogan, 1973) and speech adaptability to listeners' needs (Shatz and Gelman, 1973), but as Light (1979, p. 25) points out: "such children undoubtedly do behave egocentrically in a host of ways, but their egocentrism is far from complete and does not constitute nearly as tight a strait-jacket as has often been supposed."

The understanding of the social context and its conventions

From an early age, the developing child participates in social systems – be it the family, the school, or the peer group. Nevertheless, little research has been done on the development of the individual's concepts of social groups and systems of social interaction. One reason is the emphasis placed by students of social cognition on specifically moral reasoning and behavior. In response, Shantz (1975), Damon (1977) and Turiel (1978) have stressed the need to distinguish between the development of moral abilities and the development of social ones. In their work, they have concentrated on examining the development of social concepts, and their experimental paradigm emphasizes the need to assess the child's abilities in interactional contexts. They assume that the child's social development is influenced not only by specific others (as the classical learning tradition postulates) but also by interactions with patterns of social behavior and with social organizations. At each development point, the developing child must be viewed as constructing a workable social theory (a belief system) that is consistently modified in content and structure by the social environment. By observing social action, by communicating and being communicated with, the child gathers and creates social experience and social information. While the child constructs and reconstructs social beliefs, the social environment helps him or her act and react in ways that provide essential social information and structure.

This work on the understanding of social rules and social structure has led to the identification of four main stages in the development of children's reasoning about the social context and its rules. Shantz (1975) and Damon (1977) found that 3- and 4-year-olds reason in ways specific to the act and situation. Damon's interviews with children probed their views about violations of sex roles, table manners and stealing. The interviews suggest that rule-following at early ages is based on personal desires which justify compliance or non-compliance. After the 4th year, children acquire a global rationale of rules and social uniformity. However, this rationale consists of understanding what is good and bad without supplying any causal justification. In their 6th year, children become aware of social conventions as arbitrary uniformities that function to coordinate the actions of individuals within a social system. Thus a clear distinction between conventions and principles is recognized and conventional violations are judged as being less serious than principle violations. However, it is not until the 7th year that the organizational function of social rules is recognized. Violations of conventions are seen as clearly less serious than principle violations, but the social impact of conventional violations is fully understood.

In addition to an understanding of social rules and social conventions the child must acquire general social knowledge. In particular, he or she must acquire event knowledge (i.e. knowledge of familiar sequences which helps the child understand how persons act upon each other to produce social events) and knowledge about certain social categories (e.g. status, sex roles, etc.). How does the recognition of children's event knowledge enhance our understanding of children's communicative competence? Several different points come to mind. First, the notion of a sequentially based representation is an appropriate way to characterize the conceptual underpinnings of some of the linguistic phenomena of interest. Some of the child's communicative knowledge is inherently sequential in nature. For example, the rules for maintaining a conversation are based on the ability to deal with temporally contiguous speech events. Indeed, conversational settings, such as the telephone setting, consist of well-defined familiar sequences, such as starting a conversation with "Hello," then determining the identity of the caller and the nature of the call, followed by a variable length of discourse in which turn-taking is closely maintained, and concluding by saying "Good-bye." Second, other linguistic phenomena are linked with event knowledge indirectly. For example, Ervin-Tripp (1978a) reported that children drew heavily upon their practical reasoning, their understanding of common event sequences, to infer the appropriate action response to an indirect request. If the mother says: "Is the door open?" when she has her arms full of grocery bags, a child would open the door regardless of whether or not he or she understood the indirectness of the question. In other words, the child will open the door just because the context dictates that he or she should do so, regardless of the language used. Ervin-Tripp suggested that such redundancies in natural contexts contribute to the child's mastery of indirect requests.

Most researchers agree that young children have acquired some sort of general understanding of familiar sequences of events by the age of $3\frac{1}{2}$ or 4 years. Nelson (1981) concluded that script knowledge in young children is general in form, temporally organized, consistent over time and socially accurate. Her conclusions are based on a number of studies with children ranging in age from 3 to 8 years. The children were asked to tell "What happens if . . ." when they were engaged in familiar activities such as eating dinner or going grocery shopping. Even 3-year-old children were able to relate reasonably accurate sequences of events. According to Nelson, a child moves from a direct representation of social relationships to an increasingly more general, abstract and static representation. Similarly, Goldman (1982) interviewed 6-, 9- and 12-year-old children about their views on being friendly, getting a dog and doing chores. All the children had mastered the relevant information and the sequence of events leading to concrete situations (e.g. getting a dog). However, to more abstract situations (such as friendship), the younger children did not respond accurately. But, as Goldman pointed out, what most older children knew about friendship consisted only of additions to what most younger children knew: "Thus developmental differences in the content of the knowledge . . . appear to reflect an increase in the amount and variety of information expected by the majority of children within each age group" (Goldman, 1982, p. 301).

Concluding remarks and direction for research

The foregoing review presents the insights and limits of the research on child language development. My own research has been crafted accordingly. First, an attempt is made to conduct a more comprehensive study of the child's linguistic and conversational behavior. Thus the research focuses on the full spectrum of speech-acts and examines key dimensions of conversational exchange suggested by Grice's philosophical analysis. In addition, greater care is taken in the study of indirect speech. This includes an analysis of the various forms of indirect speech and the cognitive demands each places on the listener. Finally, an initial study is done of the hitherto neglected area of the child's comprehension of non-literality. Second, all of the foregoing analysis of language is conducted with regard to its relation to children's social development. A matter of considerable speculation, little systematic research has been devoted to the study of the relationship between these two dimensions of children's behavior. In my research, an attempt is made to explore the relationship between the children's language use and social cognitive ability at each point in their development. The focus of the social cognitive aspect of the research is on children's ability to make inferences about others and their capacity to understand social context. Third, the methods employed in my research include both studies in naturalistic settings and experimentation. For the most part, language use and conversation is studied in a naturalistic setting and social development is studied experimentally.

The overarching aim of the research is to provide a "developmental descriptive analysis" of children's language. The intended result is a fairly detailed picture of what develops when in the domain of social knowledge and communicative competence. The present study does not address any causal-analytic questions. Nor does it intend to make statements regarding the order of such developments. In other words, I do not wish to imply that social cognition is the prerequisite of language understanding or vice versa. To suggest that would simply be to misunderstand the complex interrelation between social cognition and language understanding. Moreover, I wish to heed Campbell's warning (1979) and avoid the circularity entailed in the use of facts about the nature of children's language to infer facts about social development that are in turn used to explain language development.

I claim that social knowledge and communicative competence are related, and that developments in one area facilitate developments in the other. This is done in recognition of the fact that the distinction between linguistic and social knowledge is not clear cut. Social concepts such as status and role are manifest only in the linguistic system. In this regard, it is language which is the key medium through which social distinctions are introduced to the child. Bowerman (1981, p. 153) makes the point well: "To the extent that socially important concepts can be inferred only through communicative interactions, and have no direct non-linguistic correlates, acquisition of them could not take place independently of language." It is my view that as children acquire the system of language-based knowledge, that is as they become communicatively competent, they draw upon and define the totality of their social experiences.

4 Methods of research

The research I report here has four specific goals:

(1) To investigate the kind of social functions language performs at different points in the child's development. This requires an exploration of the young child's ability to use language to make reference to objects, to make requests, to assert and to initiate conversations. It also involves an examination of the degree to which children at different developmental points are competent in producing successful speech-acts and coherent discourse.

(2) To analyze the kind of interaction in which children are able to engage. The focus here is on how the child's social interaction changes with his or her development. This is analyzed with reference to the development of the child's language use investigated in (1).

(3) To examine when and how children begin to understand the "conversational meaning" of an utterance. The aim here is to understand the interpretative process which occurs in conversational exchanges. This entails an analysis of the development of linguistic communication with respect to those inferential abilities which help young children to see conversational acts as accomplishments of social episodes.

(4) To examine the relationship between the development of children's socio-cognitive abilities and the development of their capacity to be competent conversational partners. This leads to an analysis of children's performance on certain socio-cognitive tasks as it relates to their language use and conversation as studied in (1), (2) and (3).

In this chapter, the design of the research conducted to achieve these goals is presented. Certain methodological issues are considered and then the specific methods used in the research are discussed in some detail.

Methodological considerations

The aim of investigating conversational behavior and social functioning
sets certain requirements which empirical research must be designed to
meet. First, there is the need to allow for a detailed analysis of what children
do with language and how they do it in a social context. A key concern here
revolves around the recognition that language use occurs within a social
context. This requires a research design which allows for the observation of
children's language use as it occurs in a natural everyday environment. At
the same time, the research must be designed so as to allow for detailed
observation. The understanding of conversational interaction requires a
clear picture of non-verbal as well as verbal behavior. Non-verbal cues (e.g.
eye-to-eye contact) signal important messages to conversational partners
of any age. Non-verbal behaviors are not just an accompaniment of talk
but often, and particularly at an early age, an alternative to talk (Bates *et
al.*, 1979; Ochs, 1979; McTear, 1985). Many of the children's attention-
getting and attention-drawing devices are non-verbal. It is often the case
that the child points, or touches the mother to direct her attention, or uses
gaze to establish eye contact with her. These devices are sometimes used
together with verbal ones, but are often used as substitutes. Consequently,
to omit them would be to overlook important aspects of the child's
conversational abilities. Furthermore, to detect the presence of indirect and
non-literal speech and to understand them, it is often necessary to take into
account both the context of the speech and certain non-verbal devices used
to explicate the nature of the utterance. To assure a full recording and,
following this, a careful decoding of a conversation, it is therefore necessary
to have a videotape record of the exchange.

Second, given that the purpose of the present study is to investigate
developments in social understanding, as well as developments in language
understanding, the circumstances of the conversational exchange studied
must allow for the investigation of both these understandings. In other
words, the social setting must be such that both language and social
functioning take place. To get a lifelike, but still structured, setting, a game
involving the child and an adult was selected. The game was designed such
that it requires the two players to create the rules whereby they shall play.
To succeed they must cooperate by using language. By examining the
beginning and the end of the game interaction, it is possible to study both
the ways in which participants establish and structure their discourse, and
the ways in which they arrive at agreements about social rules and social
interactional patterns.

Two related problems are relevant here. The first concerns the extent to which the game situation can provide a representative picture of children's general conversational abilities. The problems here are ones of sampling. To begin with, there is the question as to what degree participation in a game will elicit responses which are representative of the child's conversational behavior. Clearly, any situation chosen will have its intrinsic biases. The game situation was chosen both because children are familiar with such a situation and because it necessitates a considerable amount and variety of conversational behavior. In addition, there is the question as to how representative the performance of such a small group of subjects can be. This may be a problem, but at this early stage in research a detailed analysis of a relatively small sample of the children's language use is preferable to a more superficial analysis of a larger sample where many aspects of conversational behavior will necessarily be overlooked.

A second and related problem concerns the extent to which the observation of the game with the use of videotape equipment might affect the naturalness and spontaneity of the observed behavior. To overcome this problem, all but three of the children who took part in the present study were recorded in their nursery. The remainder were recorded in their home. In both cases, the surrounding was a familiar and comfortable one. To reduce the impact of the camera it was placed in a far corner of the room and was set up and running before the child entered. Most children were unaware of its presence. To create an even more natural situation, the adult chosen to play the game with the child was the child's mother. It is believed that children feel more relaxed when playing with their mother. At the same time, her involvement should increase their chance both to draw on their ordinary repertoire of behaviors and also to become meaningfully involved in the situation, thus making their behavior more likely to be representative.

Third, the aim of the research also requires an analysis of the child's social awareness and sensitivity. It was felt that the game situation was not sufficient for this purpose. In order to arrive at a representative picture of the children's social development which is independent of performance in the game task, all the children were also asked to participate in three role-taking tasks. This allows for an independent assessment of the children's social understanding. At the same time, it facilitates an examination of individual differences in social functioning within the same age group. This is especially important given the evidence that age has been suggested to be a helpful but not yet a predictive variable for social development.

General procedure of the present study

Subjects

The children were selected from four age groups. There were (a) five children aged 3;6–4;0, (b) five children aged 4;6–5;0, (c) five children aged 5;6–6;0 and (d) four children aged 6;6–7;0. The mean age of the first group was 3;7, of the second group 4;8, of the third 5;7 and of the fourth 6;9. In the first two groups there were three boys and two girls. In the third group there were three girls and two boys, and in the fourth four boys. Originally, the fourth age group had five children. However, the scores of one child in the last age group were not included in the final results. For most of the recording sessions the mother was the one to talk and this child, aware of the camera, became camera-shy. It was thus felt that his performance could not be representative of his true abilities and it was therefore not included in the present analysis. All the other children had no problems with the game situation or the social tasks.

Three children were videotaped in their own homes rather than in the nursery. Since the observer came to their house and set up the camera in front of them, they were fully aware of being videotaped. However, they did not appear to be unduly affected by the presence of the camera. From time to time they looked in the direction of it, but otherwise they ignored it and got on with their play. According to the mothers, their play did not differ substantially from other occasions when they played together without the presence of the camera.

All the children but one were selected from a particular nursery located in a middle-class community in California. All the subjects were volunteers. Initially, leaflets were distributed to all the mothers at the nursery explaining the purpose and the methodology of the study. Then the mothers interested in becoming part of the study were asked to make an appointment with the nursery coordinator.

The recording sessions

The recording sessions took place, in all but three cases, in an isolated room in the nursery. The observer had set up the camera before the child and the mother came in. As soon as the mother and child had entered the room the observer explained the purpose of the interaction and left the room. The length of the recording sessions varied with each individual mother–child pair. The average length of the sessions for the first two age groups was 20 minutes and for the last two age groups 35 minutes.

After each pair had finished the game the mother was asked to come to an adjacent room to inform the observer. Immediately after, the observer met the child and played with each child for about an hour. After this first contact, the child was asked to participate in the three socio-cognitive tasks. The mother was encouraged to be present, and most in fact were. However, four of the mothers had to leave and the socio-cognitive tasks were played without their presence.

The children's performance in the socio-cognitive tasks was recorded. The recording sessions for the socio-cognitive tasks lasted for approximately 30–40 minutes.

The game situation

The game was a board game without any specified rules. As already noted, the point was to create a game which required the players to cooperate by using language in order to arrive at an agreement about the rules of the game and then play it. The board game was designed by me. It was, however, similar to a popular game played in the United States which is called "Candyland." I believed that using a game which was somehow familiar to most children would make the situation less stressful, especially for the younger age group. All the children were familiar with "Candyland" and had played it at least once. Each mother–child pair was presented with a 35 cm × 57.5 cm game board which featured a road composed of a series of colored squares. The children had to snake their way from the beginning to arrive at a goal (a box of candies). There were several forks in the road (one was leading towards the goal and the others leading off the board). In the course of the journey the children encountered several potential threats (e.g. wild animals and witches). The complexity of the game varied according to the child's interpretation of these threatening objects. The design of the board is presented in figure 4.1.

Along with the board, the children were handed a square cube with different colors on each side (could be used as a dice), a cutout figure of a key (could be used to open the door for the candies), a cutout figure of a sword (could be used for protection from the animals), and a toy pig and cow. These objects were not necessary for the game. Their employment as parts of the game was up to the individual child.

Two adult pairs were also asked to perform the same task. Their interactions were recorded and transcribed in the same manner as the

Figure 4.1 The board game

children's. This was done to provide a standard for evaluating the children's performance on this new task.

Transcription rules

All the videotapes of each mother–child pair were transcribed. The basic transcript included information about both the verbal and the non-verbal behavior of the participants. The behavior of the child and the mother was presented side by side in parallel columns. Turns were thus separated in individual-participant columns. A portion of the actual transcript and its format is presented in figure 4.2.

The advantages of using such a format for children's transcripts are twofold (Ochs, 1979). First, the reader can more easily see the prior verbal behavior of the child. In interpreting the child's utterance, the reader of a transcript can assess its place with respect to what the child has been saying or doing as well as with respect to the talk or behavior of the other speaker. That is, the present format provides greater access to the stream of behaviors that the talk of another may have interrupted. In this way, the researcher may assess whether the child's behavior is contingent on the talk

Child		Mother		Context
Non-verbal	Verbal	Verbal	Non-verbal	
1. Looks at M.	1. We are to play it.		1. Looks at C.	M = Mother
2. Points at board.		2. Um.	2. Looks at board, comes to C.	C = Child
3. Expressionless.		(pause)	3. Looks at board, then at M.	Mother and child are sitting around the table in the nursery. The game Interaction has just begun.
4. Points at board.	4. (U)		4. Leans, looks closely at M.	
5. Watches M.		5. We can go here.	5. Points at route on board.	
6. Smiles, points at board.	6. Brown (WH)		6. Looks where C points.	
7. Watches M.		7. Brown! YES.	7. Points at brown square.	
8. Looks closely at board.		8. And *this?*	8. Points at red square.	
9. Looks at M.	9. Red.	9. //Red.	9. Looks at C, smiles.	
10. Looks at M.	10. Gre::en.		10. Looks at board.	
11. Then at board.			11. Looks at C, nods.	

Figure 4.2 An example of the transcript

of another or whether it is contingent on both or neither. Second, several studies (Keenan, 1974; Keenan and Klein, 1975) which documented the development of discourse coherence of twins over a period of one year showed that young children link their utterances to their prior talk before linking them with the speech of others. Thus verticality within each speaker column encourages such kinds of discourse links. Further studies of children at the one-word stage (Bloom, 1973; Keenan and Schieffelin, 1976; Atkinson, 1979) indicate that the expressions of a single proposition frequently cover the space of several utterances.

A third column, near the participants' columns, provides the reader with specific information about the general context of the discourse. This is particularly important in understanding the presence of indirect or non-literal expressions.

The mother's column was added on the right-hand side of the child's column with a specific purpose in mind. In this way, transcription biases do not coincide with a priori cultural biases (i.e. the mother as the competent language user who controls and dominates discourse).

As the above example indicates, behaviors are numbered sequentially as they occur. Behaviors are numbered for each page of transcription. Furthermore, as figure 4.2 shows, behaviors by two different participants that occur at the same time are numbered by the same number. This system is useful in classifying different behaviors and in clearly showing to the reader the exact overlap of non-verbal with verbal behaviors (e.g. the child's non-verbal behaviors (10) and (11), which occur within a single utterance).

Certain symbols were used to describe non-verbal actions and frames, as well as matters of timing. These symbols are explained in appendix 1. Extracts from the videotape transcripts are also presented in appendix 1.

Specific procedure of data analysis

The transcripts were analyzed in two ways. First, a language analysis was carried out. However, in order to examine how language is placed in the general interactional pattern of the participants, a socio-interactional analysis was also performed.

Language analysis

The utterances of both the child and mother were coded in relation to their function as speech-acts. A special note was made as to whether the utterances performed a direct, indirect or non-literal function. In order to investigate how well young children communicate, the children's assertions were isolated and their degree of relevancy and cooperation was examined.

Speech-acts analysis

The utterances of both participants were coded according to Bach and Harnish's classification system. Their system includes six major classes of functions: assertives, responsives, requestives, commissives, expressives and acknowledgment. Although Bach and Harnish's system is used, it was designed for the analysis of adult language. For purposes of the analysis of children's language, their classes were subdivided into a total of 20 highly differentiated subclasses of conversational acts. Part of Dore's (1977b) system was used to arrive at the 20 subcategories. The actual system used in the present study is quite different from Dore's owing to the poor interobserver agreement that was obtained with Dore's original system. The major classes with their subdivisions, together with the definition of each class, are shown below.

Speech-acts classification

Assertives
Utterances which report facts, state rules, convey attitudes, etc.

(i) Assertions about objects
(ii) Assertions about events
(iii) Assertions about internal phenomena

Responsives
Utterances which supply solicited information to a prior requestive act

(i) Replies supplying solicited information
(ii) Replies supplying extended information

Requestives
Utterances which solicit information from the hearer

(i) Real questions
(ii) Test questions
(iii) Verbal reflective questions

(iv) Requests for
    clarification
(v) Requests for action
(vi) Suggestions
(vii) Requests for
    permission

Commissives
Utterances which look
  forward and promise or
  offer a statement to the
  partner

Expressives
Non-propositional
  utterances which convey
  attitudes or repeat prior
  utterances or
  acknowledge the
  utterances of others

(i) Exclamations
(ii) Accompaniments
(iii) Repetitions
(iv) Attention-seeking
    devices

Acknowledgment
Any non-propositional
  utterance which either
  recognizes prior non-
  requestive acts or simply
  helps the maintenance of
  the conversational flow

(i) Utterance agreeing
    with or rejecting prior
    utterance
(ii) Thanks
(iii) Apologies
(iv) Congratulations or
    greetings

To this list, two more categories were added – the category of Personal speech and the category of Uninterpretables. Given that Bach and Harnish's system is for adult conversations, it is perhaps not surprising that it does not include personal or private speech. However, it was judged that such a category was needed in the present study since young children often talk to themselves and do not use language which is directed to others. These two categories are summarized below:

Personal speech
Essentially covers any speech which is apparently an
  accompaniment to an activity and apparently addressed to
  the speaker (self) rather than others.

Uninterpretables

Any utterance judged to be uncodable by the observer and any
utterance which was unintelligible at the stage of
transcription to the observer. ·

Each transcript was coded by myself. To assess the reliability of the
coding system and my use of it I employed a graduate student in
psychology. After a brief training period and the lapse of one week, the
graduate student was asked to code five randomly selected pages of
material. His coding was then compared with my own. Intercoder
reliability was assessed at 94% for the speech-acts analysis. (For a detailed
description of the definitions used for the speech-act categories and their
subcategories, see appendix 2.)

Analysis of indirect and non-literal speech

All the speech-acts produced by both the mother and the child were
examined for the degree of their directness and non-literality. The different
types of direct, indirect and non-literal speech were identified according to
the following criteria:

Indirect speech-acts

Any speech-act which was judged as having two illocutionary forces was
coded as being an indirect speech-act. To judge the presence of an indirect
speech-act, the coder had to rely on the relevant contextual information of
the utterance in question. For example:

> Speaker (S) utters: "There is a tiger there" to the hearer (H).
> It is a mutual contextual belief that S and H are playing a game and the
> location of the tiger on the board is irrelevant to the discussion so far.
> Thus H infers that S could not be merely stating that the tiger is over there.
> It is a mutual contextual belief that "tigers" are dangerous. Thus H infers
> that S, in stating that there is a tiger there, is also requesting H not to go
> near the tiger.
> Therefore the utterance "There is a tiger there" is an assertion but under
> the specific circumstances it serves an additional illocutionary intent and
> it also becomes a requestive.

All the indirect utterances were isolated and they were recoded according
to several subcategories. Following Bach and Harnish (1979) there are
three main subcategories of indirectness:

(1) *Standardized form*
Some forms which appear to be indirect actually behave as if they were direct in that the usual inferential process illustrated above is apparently short-circuited. This process has been called "standardization" and some typical examples are:
(a) *Wh-* imperatives
E.g. Could you pass the salt?
    Would you pass the salt?
Indirect force: (I request you) to pass the salt.
(b) Impositives
E.g. Why don't you read?
    Shouldn't you read?
    How about reading?
Indirect force: (I request you) to read.
(c) Queclaratives
E.g. Does anyone read anymore?
Indirect force: Nobody reads anymore.

(2) *Pragmatic idioms* (or situated conventional speech)
Some forms do not receive their proper interpretation in any regular way; they are in effect idiomatic and must be learned case by case. Here are some typical examples:
(a) Imperatives
E.g. Take it easy (calm down).
    Never mind (forget it).
    Buzz off   (leave).
(b) Interrogatives
E.g. Isn't that nice? (that's nice)
    How do you do?

(3) *Hints* (logical inferences)
Hints require a logical inference on the part of the hearer for the realization of the speaker's intention. Typical examples are "The door is over there" (implying "Leave the room") or "The matches are all gone" (Implying "Bring me some matches"). Hints are employed when the speaker and hearer can rely on shared rules or on shared understanding of habits and motives in familiar set-ups.

Non-literal speech-acts

Where it was judged that the speaker did not intend the literal meaning of the expressed phrase, the speech-act was coded as being non-literal. There are three main subcategories of non-literality. These are:

(1) *Understatement or overstatement*
E.g. Not bad! (Very good! Great!)
I wasn't born yesterday (I am not so naive).
No one understands me (Not a lot of people understand me).
In these cases, the hearer understands what is implied by recognizing the next evaluation towards the midpoint of the relevant scale.

(2) *Irony, sarcasm*
To recognize sarcastic comments, the hearer must understand that under the particular circumstances the opposite of what is said is meant.
E.g. Boy, this food is terrific! (the food is terrible)

(3) *Metaphor*
E.g. She is as tall as a tree.

For the last kind of non-literality some relation R between what is said and what is meant is needed to help guide the hearer's search for what is meant. For metaphors like "She is as tall as a tree," the R is a figurative or metaphorical connection. In most cases, such connection is learned case by case. Thus there is cultural diversity for metaphors. Whereas in our society the "tree" is used to symbolize "tallness," in another society the "house" might be used for the same purpose.

To check the reliability of the coding, agreement between observers' categorization of utterances as direct, indirect or non-literal was checked using approximately 10% of all data. Agreement was evidenced in 91% of the cases. Because of the very small number of indirect or non-literal utterances, all cases of each were used in assessing the reliability of the coder's categorization of the type of indirectness or non-literality of utterances of this kind. Intercoder agreement was assessed at 100%.

Analysis of cooperation vs uncooperation

At this level of language analysis, the focus is on the extent to which children at different developmental periods are able to draw on the relevant contextual information and make the kind of inferences required to understand each type of speech-act. To narrow down the scope of inquiry, I concentrated on two speech-act categories – assertions and responses – and analyzed them in terms of their degree of cooperation and relevance. Thus the children's assertions and responses were examined in terms of their performance and as to whether they were relevant to previous discourse.

The aim was to understand the child's communicative competence in acting upon the world. The method used for classifying cooperation and competence was influenced by suggestions in the child language literature regarding the problems that young children have in communicating. As reviewed in chapter 3, the literature suggests that the main limitation young children have in using language is in sustaining everyday communication by producing relevant replies, in clarifying their intentions and in realizing that their perspective is not always clear to others.

The following system was used to classify the child's assertions and responses:

Analysis of children's assertions

All the assertions produced by the children were isolated and were numbered. These were then coded according to specific categories. There were two main categories under which the child's assertions could fall. The assertions could be cooperative assertions or uncooperative assertions (in the case of the latter the child is talking to him- or herself and thus uses private speech).

Two subcategories of cooperative assertions were defined: successful and unsuccessful cooperative assertions. The former are assertions directed to the hearer and successful in terms of the hearer's ability to understand them. The latter are assertions which, although directed to the hearer, the hearer is not in a position to understand (e.g. the child utters "I want it" without specifying verbally or non-verbally what "it" refers to).

The successful assertions were further analyzed according to the degree to which comprehension depended on the verbal or the non-verbal general context. Thus some assertions were grouped as being made appropriate by the verbal discourse (e.g. "I like it" when "it" refers to the "doll" used in the previous utterance) and others as being made appropriate by non-verbal signals (e.g. "I want this" accompanied by pointing).

Analysis of children's responses

Given the aim of assessing the degree of successful communication within the four age groups, the children's responses were coded as successful, unsuccessful or uncooperative responses. The coding criteria were as follows:

> *Successful responses*
>   (i) directly relevant responses
>   E.g. S: What color is that?
>   H: Blue.

(ii) Indirectly relevant responses
   E.g. S: Where do you want to go?
      H: No play.
(iii) Non-verbal responses
   E.g. S: Where shall we start?
      H: (points at GO)

Unsuccessful responses
   (i) Irrelevant responses
   E.g. S: When did we play such a game?
      H: Tomorrow grandma.

Uncooperative responses
   (i) No responses
   E.g. S: What shall we do with this? (shows dice)
      H: (turns back, plays)

The intercoder reliability here was tested using 10% of all assertions and responses, and was assessed at 98%.

Analysis of social interaction

The child's behavior during the game interaction was broken down into several units. Each behavioral unit represented either a verbal utterance accompanied by a non-verbal act or a relevant non-verbal act. Each unit was then coded according to whether the unit represented an act which was positive and facilitated further interaction, or was negative and inhibited further social interaction. To be more specific, these two categories were broken down into several subcategories:

Positive social interactional acts
   (i) Initiations   (a) Labels
                             (b) Informs
                             (c) Requests
                             (d) Non-verbal
   (ii) Responses   (a) One-word
                             (b) Extended
                             (c) Non-verbal
   (iii) Shared activity   (a) Watches
                             (b) Gives
                             (c) Takes
                             (d) Smiles

                                              (e) Concentrates on same
                                                  activity
                                              (f) Acts in agreed ways, e.g.
                                                  throws dice

Negative social interactional acts
    (i) Waiting for initiation   (a) Stares at board or mother
                                        (b) Sits motionless
   (ii) Non-social behaviors   (a) Concentrates on irrelevant
                                            act
                                        (b) Acts against agreed rules
                                        (c) Talks to self
                                        (d) Cries, leaves room
                                        (e) Attempts to terminate
                                            interaction without
                                            informing partner
  (iii) Unresponsive
        behaviors   (a) Sits motionless
                                        (b) Concentrates on different
                                            activity

Intercoder reliability was assessed for judgments of whether an act was a positive or a negative one and whether it was a positive initiation, a response, or an act which indicated shared activity. The other subcategories were not checked for reliability because no statistical analysis was done on them. The reliability was assessed at 88% in the social interactional acts analysis. (For a detailed description of the social interactional act categories, see appendix 2.)

Analysis of mothers' conversational styles

In several studies it was found that mothers' speech to children is distinctively different from their speech to other adults. At the same time, there are individual differences in mothers' conversational styles (e.g. Howe, 1978; Nelson, 1973; McDonald and Pien, 1982). It is believed that differences in mothers' conversational styles may in fact create differences in the children's language use. The present analysis investigates the extent to which mothers' language across and within each age group varies. Two main issues are examined here. The first concerns the existence of any individual differences in mothers' conversational styles across and within age groups. The second considers whether the variation among mothers (if there is any) is merely a response to differential age or linguistic maturity in the children.

All the utterances produced by the mother in the game situation had been previously coded according to their illocutionary force in the speech-acts analysis. Here a further classification of the mother's intended illocutionary force was obtained. The system adopted was McDonald and Pien's (1982) category system. This system differentiates the utterances intended to elicit or acknowledge physical actions from those intended to elicit or acknowledge verbal behavior. This differentiation appears necessary because, as McDonald and Pien pointed out, a mother's conversational behavior tends to fall into two main clusters: that which elicits conversational participation and that which attempts to control and direct the child's behavior. The mother who wishes to elicit her child's conversational participation will do so through the use of frequent questions (especially low-constraint questions), infrequent negations of the child's actions, infrequent use of directives, and infrequent monologuing. On the other hand, the mother who wishes to control or direct her child's behavior will do so through the use of frequent high-constraint questions (i.e. test questions), frequent use of directives, frequent use of negations of the child's verbal or physical actions, and frequent monologuing.

To explore these kinds of functions, the speech-acts produced by the mother were further classified. Requestives were broken down into five subcategories:

(1) *Real questions*. Information-seeking questions for which the speaker does not have the answer. These types of questions carry a low degree of constraint of the child's behavior.
(2) *Test questions*. Information-seeking questions for which the speaker already has an answer. They are thus used to direct the hearer's attention, to demonstrate his or her knowledge or to explore its extent. Such questions carry a high degree of constraint.
(3) *Verbal reflective questions*. Questions which repeat, reduce or paraphrase the hearer's previous utterance, without adding new information. They often take the form of yes–no questions with rising intonation (e.g. "He did?") or tag questions with falling or falling-rising intonation (e.g. "He did, didn't he?"). Verbal reflective questions act to acknowledge the previous utterance, while at the same time they pass the speaking turn to the hearer. Their constraint upon the form or content of the hearer's response

is minimal, for what is required is only a response which maintains the conversational topic.

(4) *Clarifications*. Devices for "repairing" conversation when a misunderstanding has arisen. Repairs elicit a whole or partial repetition of the hearer's previous utterance with no alternative and are thus considered high-constraint questions.

(5) *Permission*. These questions seek permission or acceptance for an action of the speaker. These questions may be thought of as indirect commands.

The category of acknowledgment was also broken down into two categories:

(1) *Positive acknowledgment* (e.g. "Good girl!")
(2) *Negative acknowledgment* (e.g. "No" in response to the child's action)

The mother's dominance or monologuing was also measured. The degree of a mother's monologuing was measured by the mother utterance–turn ratio, that is by the average number of mother utterances in a speaking turn.

The agreement between observers was checked on 10% of all the mother utterances. The reliability was assessed at 91%.

Method and analysis of the socio-cognitive tasks

It has already been pointed out that the observer was called into the room as soon as each mother–child pair had finished with the game. The observer then played with each child for approximately an hour, and as soon as the child was familiar with the observer she administered the three socio-cognitive tasks. The child's behavior during those tasks was videotaped. The transcription, however, was not as detailed as for the game situation. The following provides an example of the running-record method used.

> Observer: What is happening to the little boy?
> Child: It is his birthday (looks at O, smiles).
> Observer: And is he giving a party? A birthday party?
> Child: (looks at O, nods head)
> Observer: How do you think he feels? (pause)
>   What's his face? (turns, looks at child)
> Child: (turns, looks at faces) Ha::ppy!

Observer: Happy. Good. Put the face on the boy.

Child: (selects happy face, puts it on top of the boy's body)

A description of the three socio-cognitive tasks is presented below.

The "guess my story" task and the "face sensitivity" task

The first task given to the children was concerned with "face sensitivity" to others' emotions and with the set of inferences needed for the child to guess what another person is trying to say by inferring the causality of pictures. In designing the task I was influenced by the work of Borke (1971, 1973) and Light (1979). Borke presented a series of short stories to children between 3 and 8 years of age. The children were asked to indicate how the child in each story felt by selecting a "happy," "sad," "cross" or "scared" face. Similarly, Light read aloud some short stories and the children were asked to select among several faces the one which they thought matched the appropriate emotion of the child in the story.

In the present study, the child was asked to generate a story which matched some pictures and then to select an appropriate face. The "guess my story" task comprised six pictures of objects and five faceless cutout figures of a boy. The cards were presented to the child in a predetermined sequence and each card represented an event. The six pictures of objects were: a birthday cake, a present, a present box partially opened, a box with a snake coming out of it, a cat eating a piece of the birthday cake, and a sick boy in bed. The pictures were presented in the following sequence: (1) a boy with his birthday cake and his present, (2) a boy who sits down and opens the present, (3) a boy who discovers a snake in the present box, (4) a boy who sees a cat eating a piece of his birthday cake and, finally, (5) a boy who is ill in bed. (An example of the pictures given to the children is presented in figure 4.3.)

I presented the pictures to each child and asked them to guess the story. As soon as the child came up with an interpretation, I asked: "Which face do you think the boy has?" or "How do you think the boy feels?" For that purpose eight colored pictures of boys' faces were drawn – two happy, two scared, two sad and two cross faces. The child was presented with two faces representing each emotion so that he or she could choose the same face for several sets of pictures if he or she thought that doing so was appropriate. Finally, the child was asked to pick up the face he or she felt was the most appropriate one and to complete the boy's faceless figure. (The faces used for this task are presented in figure 4.4.)

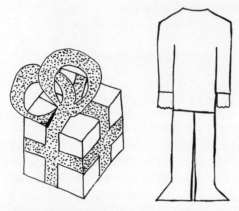

Figure 4.3 Examples of pictures from the "guess my story" task: the birthday present and the faceless boy

Figure 4.4 The four emotions used for the "face sensitivity" task

The "hiding" task

As soon as the children had completed the "guess my story" task and the task of "face sensitivity," a "hiding" task was presented. This was a variation of Light's (1979) task which aimed to explore the child's ability in role-taking. In my version, the task focused on a three-dimensional figure of a cat and a picture of a birthday cake. The goal was to hide the cake

Figure 4.5 The "hiding" task

from the cat by placing it among a group of obstacles arranged for that purpose. The obstacles were a two-dimensional wall, a three-dimensional armchair and a three-dimensional table. The child was asked to "hide the cake so that the cat cannot see it." When the child had done so, the child was given the cat figure and asked: "Can the cat see the cake?" If the child answered "No," he or she was then asked to take the cat and to find the cake. The same procedure was carried out with a boy figure, a girl figure and a doll figure replacing the cat and a doll replacing the cake. In each of the four trials, the positions of the wall, armchair and table were changed. (The task is illustrated in figure 4.5.)

Scoring

To score the socio-cognitive tasks, I initially adopted Light's (1979) system. He developed a set of four- or five-point categorical scales. However, when applying these to the analysis of our children's performance, I found them inadequate. Most of the children's performance scores fell into the middle two of Light's categories. To develop a more sensitive measure, I expanded Light's scoring categories by differentiating the middle categories. For example, in the "hiding" task I observed that there were important differences in the quality of the major errors committed as well as their number. The $4\frac{1}{2}$-year-old and 5-year-old children committed only one kind of major error in hiding the object from another person's view. They hid the object under the table. Although the object can be seen, there is a clear attempt to hide the object. The $3\frac{1}{2}$-year-old and 4-year-old children committed cruder errors. For example, they "hid" the cake in the middle of the room and merely turned the head of the seeker doll (replacing the cat) to the side. Using my eight-category measure, I was able to code these differences.

Applying my expanded measure, I was still dissatisfied. The categorical system was not doing justice to the richness of the data. Subtle, but important, distortions were produced. The key problem was that, although the categories defined a series of steps in the ever more adequate solving of a task, there were clear differences in the cognitive level accomplished in moving from one step to the next. To refine the measure further, the qualitative categories were translated into a percentage scale which more accurately reflected the relative distances between the developmental steps.

The advantage of my scale may be illustrated with reference to the "guess my story" task. Using the categorical measure, I could only note that children progressed from (a) being unable to perform the task, to (b) giving a label in response to the question "What is that?", to (c) giving the label by themselves, to (d) giving a description of the objects, to (e) describing the event, to (f) giving a descriptive story, and so on. The conceptual (and later, statistical) problem is that each of these steps is regarded as an equivalent increment of achievement. Using the 0–100 scale, I could represent my sense of the relative distance between the steps. I assigned only 5-point differences between minor advances such as giving a label on one's own rather than just in response to the experimenter's inquiry. I assigned a much larger increase (15 points) when the child takes the very significant step from describing the events in each picture to offering a descriptive story which integrates the four pictures.

Another example of the advantage of my interval scale is provided by the "hiding" task. In scoring this task, I wished to differentiate between major errors. In particular, I felt that the error of "hiding under the table" reflected more adequate performance than the others. However, I did not wish to overestimate this difference. Other distinctions among categories reflect greater progress. By using the 0–100 scale, I was able both to differentiate the "hiding under the table" error from the others and to indicate that it reflected a relatively minor advance. Interobserver agreement was checked. It was evidenced in 87% of the cases.

In sum, I decided to score the socio-cognitive tasks using a measure which transposed my expanded eight-category system onto a 100-point scale. It is certainly the case that my assignment of relative distances between categories is somewhat arbitrary and vulnerable to criticism.

However, I felt the advantages outweighed the disadvantages. Armed with an interval scale, I was able to measure the performance of subjects in a way which was more sensitive to the differences between them. This in turn allowed for a more powerful statistical analysis of our results and ultimately a more accurate portrayal of the children's behavior.

The "guess my story" task was scored as follows:

Points 0: The child is unwilling to participate.

Points 25: The child is unable to perform.

Points 30: The child seems unable to come up with a story-like elaboration of the six pictures. However, the child answers experimenter's questions of the form "What is that?"

Points 35: The child names particular objects in the picture (e.g. "A snake").

Points 45: The child gives a description for each picture after the experimenter's questions (e.g. "A cake and a boy").

Points 55: The child labels the events that are represented in each picture (e.g. "Birthday party"). However, there is no attempt to link the pictures or to use any connective or anaphoric articles.

Points 70: The child gives a more or less straightforward presentation of the six-picture story. The story includes some connective articles (e.g. "and", "then") but is very descriptive and lacks motivational statements of any kind. The child simply describes the objective details of the situation or action.

Points 90: The child gives an elaborated story of the six pictures. However, the child comes up with the story with the experimenter's help.

Points 100: The child offers an elaborated story. The presentation of the correct six-picture story makes it obvious that in the child's mind one picture represents an event which has a place in a sequence. The story includes motivational statements and connective and anaphoric articles.

The "face sensitivity" task was scored in the following manner:

Points 0:   The child is unwilling to participate in the task.

Points 25:   The child is unable to perform.

Points 35:   The child comes up with emotions which match the story but seems unable in more than half of the trials to find the appropriate face to match the emotion.

Points 40:   The child uses the "happy" face improperly.

Points 50:   More than one "sad," "scared" and "cross" face is used inappropriately, with or without the right emotion.

Points 65:   Only one "sad," "scared" and "cross" face is used inappropriately, with or without the right emotions.

Points 75:   The appropriate emotion is chosen and the face to match the emotion is selected, but the child makes one careless identification of faces, which is corrected.

Points 90:   Fully correct choices in all six trials. The appropriate emotion is chosen and the face to match the emotion is selected. However, in at least two trials the child comes up with his or her choice only after the experimenter's query "How does the child feel?"

Points 100: Fully correct choices in all six trials. The appropriate emotion is chosen and the right face to match the emotion is selected without the experimenter's questioning.

The scoring categories for the "hiding" task were the following:

Points 0:   The child is unwilling to participate.

Points 25:   The child shows interest in the game and seems unable to perform.

Points 30:   The child makes more than one major error or errors of some kind in all trials. Major errors were such that the object supposedly hidden was in fact openly and immediately visible to the seeker doll.

Points 45: The child makes one major error other than hiding the object under the table.

Points 50: The child makes one major error. In this category, however, the major error performed was only of one kind. The object was hidden under the table.

Points 60: The child makes two or three minor errors or at least one minor error which was left uncorrected or was corrected only after the experimenter's query "Will that be a good hiding place?" or "Are you sure that the cat cannot see the cake?" Minor errors included careless placements (e.g. leaving an arm or a foot of the hidden doll (replacing the cake) protruding), or placements behind an armchair or the wall which did not use the limited cover effectively.

Points 70: One or two minor errors otherwise all correct. These errors were spontaneously corrected by the child.

Points 80: No errors in all four trials. The child in more than two of the trials placed the object in a position where both the seeker doll and the child could not see it.

Points 100: No errors in all four trials. In more than two of the trials the child placed the object in a position where the doll could not see it but the child could.

5 Evidence on language use

The game interaction discussed in chapter 4 provided the primary data on children's language use. In this chapter the results of the analysis of this data are presented and then placed in the context of other work on child language development. To begin, there is a report of the data on the speech-acts produced by mother and child for each of the four age groups together with an analysis of the differences of the number, type of use, success and directness of the speech-acts across the age groups. This is followed by a discussion of the results of the research on indirectness and non-literality. The chapter closes with a discussion of the evidence on conversational cooperation.

Speech-acts analysis

Each utterance addressed to the child or the mother during the game interaction was coded according to the conversational act or function it performed. The coding system itself is presented in chapter 4. Then, for each age group, the mean number of conversational acts of each conversational class and a standard deviation within the age group was computed for both the mothers and the children. The results suggest that despite some within-group variability, the speech-acts produced by the children and their mothers differ across age groups.[1] The relationship between the mothers' and the children's scores was also examined. A non-significant relationship was found between the mothers' and the children's acknowledgments $(r=0.29)$, commissives $(r= -0.152)$, expressives $(r= -0.009)$, assertives $(r= -0.008)$, requestives $(r=0.01)$ and responsives $(r=0.39)$. The nature and extent of these sets of differences will be analyzed further in the discussion which follows. I begin with the differences between children of different ages and then compare the children with their mothers.

Functions that language performs at different developmental periods

The distribution of functions within general conversational class is presented in table 5.1. The table presents the total number of utterances of each class and the percentage this represents of all the utterances made by the children of each age group and by their mothers.

The data presented in table 5.1 indicate interesting differences both in the child's language use across the four age groups and between the child's language use and that of the mother. As far as the child's language use is concerned, the results suggest that all the children were able to use language to perform a variety of functions. All were able to use language to request, to make a statement, to respond and to acknowledge prior utterances. The overall pattern of the child's language use remains more or less the same across the four age groups. The use of assertives is most frequent for all children. The second most frequent function is the use of responsives. Commissives are the category of language used least by all the age groups and not at all by the children of the first age group. Commissives are utterances that look forward and promise or offer a statement to the hearer committing the speaker to some future course of action. Both Searle (1969) and Bach and Harnish (1979) have commented on the fact that this kind of speech-act is the hardest one to find in everyday conversations. However, the context of the game is ideal for the employment of such language uses because it encourages language which is directed to future actions. It seems, therefore, that the actual illocutionary force of such utterances is too complicated for the younger children. Additionally, it is important to note that only in the first age group was there substantial evidence of private speech. Children between the ages of $3\frac{1}{2}$ and 4 are more likely to use speech to fulfill their personal needs than older children. In contrast, older children's utterances were used only as a social activity, where conversational participation becomes the main aim and purpose of language.

Despite these similarities in the functions that language performs, there are important differences across the four age groups. Significant differences were found among the general conversational classes and among the several subcategories within each conversational class. We have a decrease of responsives (from 27.5% to 18.9%) with age, accompanied by an increase in requestives and expressives (from 8.2% to 15.7% and from 4.5% to 8.5% respectively). More significant are the differences across the age groups in the functions of language for the subcategories of the major conversational classes – the assertives, responsives and requestives. An analysis of each of these classes will be presented in turn.

Table 5.1. *Distribution of functions within general conversational class*

	Age group 1 Mean age: 3;7		Age group 2 Mean age: 4;8		Age group 3 Mean age: 5;7		Age group 4 Mean age: 6;9	
	Child	Mother	Child	Mother	Child	Mother	Child	Mother
Assertives	109 40.5%	157 33.5%	185 36.4%	134 22.4%	187 40.6%	202 38.5%	180 38.3%	161 35.7%
Responsives	74 27.5%	5 1%	138 27.2%	14 2.3%	89 19.3%	17 3.2%	89 18.9%	38 8.4%
Requestives	22 8.2%	192 40.3%	51 10%	243 40.6%	65 14.4%	159 30.3%	74 15.7%	128 28.4%
Commissives	— —	8 1.7%	5 1.0%	4 0.7%	7 1.5%	4 0.8%	10 2.1%	3 0.7%
Expressives	12 4.5%	37 7.8%	35 6.9%	49 8.2%	38 8.2%	50 9.5%	40 8.5%	40 8.9%
Acknowledgment	20 7.4%	65 13.7%	53 10.4%	137 23.0%	46 10.0%	67 12.8%	56 11.9%	70 15.5%
Uncodable	17 6.3%	11 2.3%	38 7.5%	17 2.8%	28 6.1%	26 5.0%	21 4.5%	10 2.2%
Personal	15 5.6%	— —	3 0.6%	— —	— —	— —	— —	— —
Total	269	475	508	598	460	525	470	450

Table 5.2. *Distribution of the children's assertives into three subcategories*

	Labeling	Descriptions of events	Statements about internal events	Total
Age group 1 (3;6–4;0)	60.0 (55.0%)	21 (19.3%)	28 (25.7%)	109
Age group 2 (4;6–5;0)	43 (23.2%)	58 (31.3%)	84 (45.4%)	185
Age group 3 (5;6–6;0)	41 (21.9%)	110 (58.9%)	36 (19.2%)	187
Age group 4 (6;6–7;0)	25 (13.9%)	93 (51.7%)	62 (34.4%)	180

Assertion is that function in which language is used as a means of communicating information to someone who does not already possess that information. Table 5.2 presents the numbers and percentages of the remarks belonging to the different subcategories within the assertive category. The first stage of the child's attempt to talk about the world consists of his or her learning the conventional aspects of language. The first age group scored a high percentage for the labeling category. Of all assertions 55% consisted of one word which was the label of an object (e.g. "Ball") or the label of an attribution of an object (e.g. "Blue"). However, this labeling decreases with age. By age 7, only 13.9% of the child's assertive remarks were labels. Instead, assertive comments usually provided descriptions of events. Mitchell-Kernan and Kernan (1977) and McShane (1980) found that labeling is the first activity to be grasped. For 2- and $2\frac{1}{2}$-year-olds, the majority of assertive utterances are commonly labeling. By the age of 3, children begin to produce assertions which do not only label objects but also attribute properties to objects or describe an action (e.g. "Fall down"). Though our youngest group produced many labels compared to the older groups, they were still able to produce assertions which were describing events or properties of objects in 45% of the cases. Thus their speech had improved beyond that of the 2-year-olds.

With age, there is a gradual increase of vocabulary. Words that describe events and subjective feelings are acquired as is the gradual ability to produce structured utterances. There is also an increased ability to use sentences that go beyond the here and now. The use of language to refer to spatially and temporally remote phenomena is a complex cognitive and linguistic skill. Ervin-Tripp (1979) suggests that children begin to master it after their 3rd year. However, in my study, there was no evidence of any use of assertions by the $3\frac{1}{2}$-year-old children which attempted to go beyond the present environment. I only observed the beginning of this ability in our second age group. It was after the 4th year that I found children exploiting the semantic potentials of language to refer beyond the immediate context. I observed frequent instances of recall of past events or internal feelings, sometimes prompted and sometimes not. Some of the instances made reference to potential events (see example 1) or past events (see example 2).

> Example 1 Child (4;9): Let's play it again.
> Mother: You want to win?
> Child: Yes. This time I'll win.

> Example 2 Child (6;6): It is like the game I play with Kim.
> Mother: Yes, it's like Candyland.

Examining the subcategories of the child's responsives across the four age groups, there is evidence of developments similar to those found in the analysis of their assertives. Table 5.3 presents the numbers and percentages of the children's remarks which fell into the category of responsives.

As table 5.3 illustrates, responses providing only the specifically required information decreased with age. This was accompanied by an increase of responses providing extended replies. Whereas both the above types of answers are appropriate for conversation, extended replies serve an additional role. Apart from providing an answer, they also help maintain conversation by initiating further remarks and by extending the topic. Most of the minimal replies consisted of yes–no answers or naming answers.

The prevalence of minimal replies in the young child's language can be explained by taking into account many different factors. First, one can argue that the linguistic ability required for a one-word reply is substantially less than that required for an extended one. Whereas the former requires knowledge of only the conventional aspects of language, the latter needs semantic, syntactic and social ability. Second, the mother's speech towards the young children contains many instances of yes–no and naming questioning. This is not true of her speech towards older children. It seems that most mothers adapt their speech pattern according to their perception of what the young child can understand. Most mothers were aware that addressing complicated questions (e.g. those requiring explanations, justifications or extra information) would cause a breakdown of communication. Consequently, they rarely used them. Most questions, however, addressed to older children (especially toward 6-and 7-year-old children) were of a *how*, *where* and *why* nature.

Table 5.3. *Distribution of the children's responsives into two subcategories*

	One-word responses	Extended responses	Total
Age group 1 (3;6–4;0)	57 (77.0%)	17 (23.0%)	74
Age group 2 4;6–5;0	83 (61.5%)	52 (38.5%)	135
Age group 3 (5;6–6;0)	58 (65.2%)	31 (34.8%)	89
Age group 4 (6;6–7;0)	41 (46.1%)	48 (53.9%)	89

Some interesting differences among the yes–no replies of children of different ages were found. In adult conversations, yes–no questions elicit a range of alternative replies. These include yes–no replies or their equivalent, and replies containing various degrees of inferential distance between explicit answers and explanations depending on shared assumptions. For an example of the latter, the question "Can I go outside?" could be responded to with "It is cold." Such inferential gaps are in fact characteristic of communication where both the sharing of assumptions and abbreviations are considered normal.

For the first two age groups, all yes–no replies were very explicit, with an increase of explicitness in the second age group. It seems that children in the age range of $4\frac{1}{2}$ to 5 are far more preoccupied with the clarity of their responses than in saving time in replying. It was in the last two age groups that we observed a few instances of non-explicit replies to yes–no questions which depended on shared assumptions for inference (see examples 3 and 4).

Example 3 Mother: Can I go there?
          Child (6;8): You will be eaten.

Example 4 Mother: Shall we have this rule?
          Child (6;0): Ok, let's have it.

Table 5.4 presents the numbers and percentages of the child's remarks which were scored as various subcategories of the directive and requestive function. Young children rarely employed this function. Moreover, whenever they did, it was only for the purpose of soliciting an action. We have very few instances of real questioning in the youngest age group. With the second age group, on the other hand, we observe the beginning of the

Table 5.4. *Distribution of the children's requestives into seven subcategories*

	DAR	DAS	QC	QR	QT	QRF	QP	Total
Age group 1 (3;6–4;0)	16 (72.7%)	—	—	6 (27.3%)	—	—	—	22
Age group 2 (4;6–5;0)	20 (39.2%)	5 (9.8%)	9 (17.6%)	12 (23.5%)	—	2 (3.9%)	3 (5.9%)	51
Age group 3 (5;6–6;0)	19 (29.2%)	7 (10.8%)	6 (9.2%)	29 (44.6%)	—	2 (3.2%)	2 (3.1%)	65
Age group 4 (6;6–7;0)	21 (28.4%)	6 (8.1%)	5 (6.7%)	34 (45.9%)	—	2 (2.7%)	6 (8.1%)	74

Notes: DAR = Request for action
DAS = Suggestions
QC = Request for clarification
QR = Real questions
QT = Test questions
QRF = Verbal reflective questions
QP = Requests for permission

child's ability to use directives for a variety of purposes: to clarify the speaker's intention, to ask permission, to request further information and to control the information received.

Most researchers have argued that the acquisition of requestives appears earlier than the acquisition of assertives. This is because the two speech-acts are importantly different. Utterances which make a statement or an assertion are the linguistic expression of the child's cognition of the world of objects and of other people. To express successfully the speaker's intention, such utterances require conventional lexical content, whereas appropriate intonation is often sufficient to indicate a request regardless of the phonological or lexical content of the utterance. The difference goes yet further. There are behavioral correlates of requesting and directing attention such as "reaching" and "pointing" which serve to further clarify communicative intentions. These, however, cannot be behaviorally disambiguated to the same extent as statements. An additional difference between the two types of speech-acts is reflected in the fact that statements that assert are subject to criteria of truth or falsity, whereas utterances that request and call attention are more appropriately considered as felicitous or infelicitous. Thus with assertives the burden of intelligibility is carried by the semantic content of the utterance, whereas with requestives this is carried by the social and contextual conditions of the conversation. Consequently my finding of a high percentage of assertives and a smaller percentage of requestives, especially in the speech of the young children, requires an explanation which must come outside the field of the child's linguistic ability.

The present results can be explained with reference to the structure of the interaction that existed between the mother and the child as they attempted to establish the specific rules for the game. The interaction between the mothers and young children was unequal and pedagogical in nature. Mothers typically asked questions and directed behavior, while the children labeled objects around them or responded to the questions addressed to them. It is only in the last age group that a more equal interaction emerges. Here there is an increase in assertives accompanied by a rise of directives (see table 5.1). This changes the pattern of the distribution of language functions. The mother becomes a true participant with equal rights rather than a controlling figure responsible for directing communication.

Comparison of mothers' and children's speech-acts during game interactions

When we compare mothers' speech with that of their children, it becomes apparent that the mother–child interaction gradually becomes more equal as the child grows older. To begin with, this equalization is evidenced by the relative amount of speaking done by mother and child across the four age groups. In the case of the children of the youngest age group, there is a statistically significant difference between the mother's talkativeness and that of the child (Neuman-Keuls test, $NK = 3.16$, $p < 0.05$). For the remaining three age groups, this difference was not significant. This suggests that mothers of young children talk far more than their children and take greater responsibility for maintaining the conversational flow. As the children get older, however, they become increasingly able to participate verbally.

Evidence of the gradual equalization of the interaction is also provided by the data on the differences in the "uses" of language by an adult and a child across the four age groups. This is presented in table 5.1. Especially in the first two age groups, mothers typically direct actions and ask questions. In this context, it should come as no surprise that the child's level of responsives is high. With an increase in the child's age, we see a decrease in the mother's requestives (from 40.3% to 28.4%) and a move towards other uses of language. The main change in the mother's speech is in the responsives and requestives categories. The changes of these two categories come at different developmental ages. The biggest change in the mother's use of requestives is between the second and the third age group (from 40.6% to 30.3%). In the case of the mother's use of responsives, the biggest change is between the third and the fourth age group (from 3.2% to 8.4%).

Several analyses of variance were performed to determine if any of the differences between the mothers' and children's speech within each conversational class were statistically significant. A non-significant difference was found in the number of assertives produced by the mother and the child across the four age groups ($F = 0.32$, $p < 0.05$). However, a highly significant difference was found between the number of responsives used by the child and the mother across the four age groups ($F = 31.84$, $p < 0.05$). Looking at the mean scores for language use of mother and child presented in tables A and B (see pp. 153–4), we can see that mothers used significantly fewer responsives in their speech than did their children. A significant result ($F = 3.24$, $p < 0.05$) was also obtained across the four age groups. In other words, as children grow older, their use of responses increases.

The two-way analysis of variance for determining any differences in directives between the mother and child across the four age groups indicated a significant interaction effect between the age group to which the child belongs and their production of requestives ($F = 3.04$, $p < 0.05$). Looking at the mean scores, we see that children's use of directives does appear to increase with time. A comparison of means indicated that children's production of requestives in the fourth age group is significantly different from children's production in the first age group. Among the intermediate age groups, the differences between the means were not statistically significant. Even though the intermediate groups are not significantly different, they nonetheless show an increase in the expected direction. As the children grow older, their use of requestives in communicating with their mothers increases. The Neuman-Keuls test yields non-significant differences in the mother's production of requestives across the four age groups. Thus the amount of requestives in the mother's speech remains more or less constant across the age groups. A non-significant result was obtained between and within conditions for the remaining conversational classes.

Overall, across the four age groups, there are differences in how the children speak and are spoken to. In particular, mothers of young children speak more and their speech is directed to control their children's behavior. As the children grow older they become more competent in using language as a successful communicative device. Thus the actual number of speech-acts of older children increases. At the same time, older children are able to shape and control conversation by requesting and producing information relevant to the mothers' requests. This suggests that the game situation creates a context which encourages different kinds of interaction between children of different ages and their mothers. For the 4-year-old child, the interaction is quite asymmetrical – it is an exchange between a superordinate figure and a subordinate one. In contrast, for the 7-year-olds, the interaction that they are engaged in with their mothers is symmetrical.

The same conclusion can be reached by examining certain other features of the mother's conversational style. In analyzing mothers' conversational style, all the utterances produced by the mothers in the game situation were isolated and coded according to their illocutionary force. The new coding system differentiated the utterances intended to elicit or acknowledge the child's physical actions from those intended to elicit or acknowledge the child's verbal behavior.

Table 5.5. *Variation among mothers on selected conversational measures (%)*

Mother	Age group 1 (3;6–4;0)					Age group 2 (4;6–5;0)					Age group 3 (5;6–6;0)					Age group 4 (6;6–7;0)				
	1	2	3	4	5	1	2	3	4	5	1	2	3	4	5	1	2	3	4	5
Requisitives	13.2	12.7	3.7	10.0	9.4	12.5	3.2	3.8	13.8	8.5	5.7	0.9	4.6	5.5	2.4	3.6	4.0	15.2	2.8	6.4
Real questions	8.8	5.1	29.6	17.1	6.5	6.2	11.9	14.1	21.5	15.4	19.0	6.6	24.6	32.2	7.4	14.5	9.1	6.5	20.7	12.7
Test questions	8.8	4.2	3.7	3.0	3.5	9.4	1.2	0.9	4.6	6.9	—	—	1.5	3.7	—	—	—	4.3	—	1.1
Verbal reflective questions	3.3	7.7	8.6	9.0	3.5	9.4	12.5	4.7	8.5	7.7	6.7	2.8	4.6	4.0	—	1.8	10.1	4.3	2.8	4.7
Clarification	5.5	0.8	—	3.0	—	3.1	2.4	7.5	3.1	4.6	4.8	3.8	3.1	3.9	2.4	—	7.1	8.6	1.9	3.1
Permission	4.4	8.8	—	—	—	3.1	0.6	—	1.5	0.8	—	0.9	—	—	—	—	1.0	0.7	—	0.4
Positive acknowledgement	3.3	12.1	11.1	12.0	9.4	6.2	20.8	11.3	13.8	13.8	12.4	11.3	21.5	9.4	9.0	19.1	21.1	21.7	18.9	20.2
Negative acknowledgement	2.2	6.8	2.5	8.0	5.9	6.2	11.3	15.1	6.1	10.2	6.7	3.8	10.8	3.1	6.5	5.4	4.0	1.4	3.8	3.6
Assertives	31.9	37.3	28.4	28.0	37.6	28.1	20.8	22.6	26.9	23.8	36.2	39.6	38.5	25.2	53.3	32.7	30.3	41.3	35.8	35.0
Expressives	14.3	7.6	2.5	8.0	15.9	7.8	8.3	16.0	3.1	0.8	5.7	18.9	13.8	9.4	13.9	19.1	11.1	0.7	6.6	9.4
Mother dominance	1.8	3.2	0.9	2.4	5.6	1.8	1.0	0.8	1.4	1.5	0.8	2.6	0.9	2.1	1.0	1.2	1.0	0.9	0.0	0.8

Notes: The above percentages were taken from the overall utterances produced by the mothers. The categories of commissives, private speech and uncodable speech were omitted from the above table. Therefore, the percentages do not add up to 100%. Mother dominance was measured by the mother utterance–turn ratio.

Table 5.5 presents the pattern of distribution among categories across the mothers.Variability across the patterns of distribution among the mothers is not pronounced. Most mothers across the age groups used a lot of questions and a lot of assertives in communicating with their children. The third most frequent category used by mothers is the directive category together with the positive acknowledgment category.

Although there is no variation in the pattern of speech distribution among mothers in the same age group, there is an interesting variation in the use of mothers' questions and in mothers' dominance across age groups. Several analyses of variance were performed to test for any significant differences in the types of questions asked by mothers across the four age groups. It was found that mothers' speech to young children contains significantly more test questions than their speech to older children ($F=4.81$, $p<0.05$). At the same time, mothers tend to dominate the conversations with young children by producing significantly more utterances per speaking turn than they do when conversing with older children ($F=3.59$, $p<0.05$). These analyses suggest that the observed variation in mothers' conversational styles was merely a response to differential age or linguistic maturity of the children rather than a response to individual differences of children or mother styles. Most mothers adapt their language use according to their perception of their child's understanding. When they interact with young children their role is pedagogical. This is evidenced by the mother's use of a high percentage of test questions and tag questions, which serve the sole function of directing the child's attention and sustaining conversation. With an increase of age, however, the maintenance of conversation does not rest solely on the mother's skill and thus her regulatory role decreases.

To summarize, the descriptive analysis of the children's and mothers' uses of language shows that all participating children had an adequate grasp of the language and were able to use it as a powerful tool for communicating with their mothers. Even the children in the youngest age group were adequate communicators. They were able to understand most speech addressed to them, had clear intentions to communicate and, in most cases, were able to do so. Despite these accomplishments, we found that the language use of $3\frac{1}{2}$-year-old and $4\frac{1}{2}$-year-old children was limited, serving only a restricted number of functions (mainly assertions and responses). With age, the use of responsives decreased and there was an increase in requestives and expressives. Meanwhile, assertive remarks became more sophisticated than simply labeling objects, and responses became more extended. These language accomplishments had important consequences for the mother–child interaction. Whereas the mother–child interactions of the youngest age group were dominated by the mother, the mother–child interactions of the two oldest age groups were not. As the children grew older, they shared in the control over the shape and direction of conversation to a greater extent and thus became equal participants in the exchange.

Indirectness and non-literality in children's speech

Indirect and non-literal speech-acts were infrequent for all age groups. Given the low incidence of both those types of speech-acts one concern was whether the game situation itself inhibited the expression of indirect and non-literal speech. To test for this, I administered the task to one adult pair and videotaped their interaction. The pair consisted of two adults who were very familiar with each other. The degree of familiarity between adult participants was judged to be of great importance because most of the complex forms of indirectness are employed when the speakers can rely on shared understandings of habits and motives. The analysis yielded interesting findings. Familiar adults do in fact engage in complex speech-acts and depend heavily on the context for disambiguating them. Both adults engaged in producing indirect or non-literal speech 36.6% of the time. Moreover, 52.3% of all the instances of indirect remarks were implicit indirect ones (i.e. hints).

The videotaped analysis of the adult interactions showed that understanding starts from context. When the hearer is attending to ongoing action, it is possible to understand a congruent speech-act with minimal interpretative form. For example, the utterance "We are wasting time, Shawn!" (uttered with exasperation) is immediately recognized as a protest rather than first as a statement and then a protest. Thus the literal interpretation of the utterance is not likely to be considered at all because the actual context itself makes it redundant. Thus, as Ervin-Tripp (1981, p. 207) has argued: "participants become aware of inferential processes when there is an incongruity or misunderstanding . . . [although] this awareness has been the model for standard interpretation. Most of the time, language is facilitative to ongoing event projection, and merely confirms or supplements what is already known."

Such an analysis of the conversation of adults in the game situation suggests that the situation does not in fact inhibit the production of complex speech. In negotiating the rules of the game, adults used speech which did not explicitly state the desired goal or which was of a metaphoric

Table 5.6. *Numbers and proportions of direct and indirect or non-literal speech-acts*

		Direct	Indirect	Non-literal	Total
Age group 1	Mother	451 (94.9%)	21 (4.4%)	3 (0.6%)	475
(3;6–4;0)	Child	264 (98.1%)	4 (1.5%)	1 (0.4%)	269
Age group 2	Mother	560 (94.5%)	28 (4.7%)	10 (1.6%)	598
(4;6–5;0)	Child	495 (97.4%)	8 (1.6%)	5 (1.0%)	508
Age group 3	Mother	484 (92.4%)	31 (5.9%)	9 (1.7%)	524
(5;6–6;0)	Child	451 (97.0%)	10 (2.1%)	4 (0.9%)	465
Age group 4	Mother	377 (83.9%)	46 (10%)	26 (5.7%)	449
(6;6–7;0)	Child	425 (89.7%)	38 (8.0%)	11 (2.3%)	474

or sarcastic nature 36.6% of the time. Bearing this in mind, we can now proceed with the analysis of children's and mothers' indirect and non-literal speech.

The proportions of direct and indirect or non-literal speech are presented in table 5.6, which shows the total number of utterances produced by the mothers and children (five pairs) in each age group. It indicates that there is indeed a gradual increase of indirectness across the age groups, although it must be remembered that the instances of complex speech-acts were few among the first three age groups. This increase is present in both the mother's and the child's speech. Table 5.6 also shows an increase in the amount of non-literal speech, but this increase is evident only in the last age group.

A detailed analysis of the child's and the mother's indirect speech across the four age groups is presented in table 5.7. Figures 5.1, 5.2 and 5.3 present graphical representations of the same results.

Table 5.6 and figures 5.1, 5.2 and 5.3 show that there is indeed a gradual increase of indirectness across the age groups. This is evident in both the mother's and the child's speech. Two points are of interest here. First, the first three age groups evidenced similar levels of indirectness. A noticeable increase was only found in the case of the oldest group. The percentage of indirect speech for the first three age groups was 1.5%, 1.6% and 2.1% respectively. For the oldest group, it was 8.0%. It seems, therefore, that only 6½-year-old and 7-year-old children can employ more complicated language uses in their everyday conversation. Second, the mother's speech follows the pattern of the child's speech. Looking again at tables 5.6 and 5.7, we can see that the mother's indirect comments in the youngest group

Table 5.7. *Frequencies of different types of indirectness in mothers' and
children's speech*

		Standardized			Pragmatic	Hints	Total
		Wh- imperatives	Imposi- tives	Quecla- ratives			
Age group 1	Mother	9	7	—	1	4	21
(3;6–4;0)	Child	—	—	—	—	4	4
Age group 2	Mother	8	11	—	5	4	28
(4;6–5;0)	Child	—	1	—	5	2	8
Age group 3	Mother	3	9	—	9	10	31
(5;6–6;0)	Child	—	1	—	3	6	10
Age group 4	Mother	6	11	—	8	21	46
(6;6–7;0)	Child	2	7		8	21	38

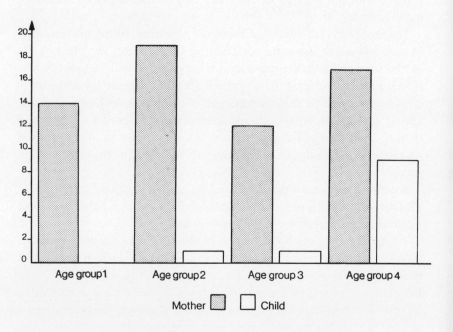

Figure 5.1 Mothers' and children's standardized indirectness

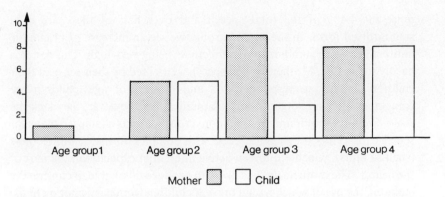

Figure 5.2 Mothers' and children's pragmatic indirectness

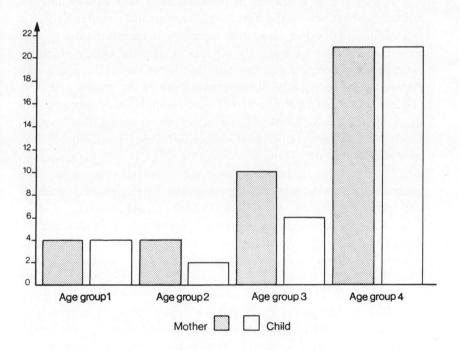

Figure 5.3 Mothers' and children's hints

represent 4.4% of the total speech and over half of these are of a standardized form. In the second group, we see an increase of pragmatic indirectness, with standardized indirectness being very high. This result is hardly surprising. Mothers' use of speech is oriented by their sense of their children's ability to respond. At 3 and 4 years of age, children are competent in using language for communicating. However, they lack the socio-cognitive requirements to see conversational acts as steps in plans for social ends. Thus they cannot cope with complex forms of indirectness (such as hints), which require an active inferential capacity on the part of the hearer. The mothers are less likely to produce talk liable to confuse the children, the use of which would prevent children from participating in the conversation. By ages 4 and 5, however, the children understand that there is a distinction between the "form" and the "function" of an utterance and they recognize that utterances of the same form may convey different attitudes and perform various functions. Therefore indirect speech which is of a standardized form is easier to comprehend. In the last two age groups, we see an increase of hints. By 6 years of age, the child's ability to understand indirectness develops fully and he or she starts coping with hints without needing explicit characterizations of the desired goal.

When examining the frequencies of the different kinds of indirectness in the children's speech, I looked first at standardized speech, that is speech which contains *wh-* imperatives, impositives and queclaratives. This speech is very simple. Though it appears indirect, it actually behaves as direct speech. This is because the usual inferential process is short-circuited. It should be expected, therefore, that indirectness of a standardized form would be the most frequent of the indirect remarks.

Investigating standardized indirectness (see table 5.7), I found that the first three age groups produced no or only one instance of standardized speech. To understand this result properly, two points should be kept in mind. First, most standardized indirectness consists of a request of the *would, should* or *why* form. But, as already mentioned, when interacting with their mothers in the game situation young children are unlikely to produce many remarks of an interrogative nature. The ability to perform a request for information implies that the speaker can exercise power and can initiate further conversation. Given the fact that the young child is an unequal participant in the social interaction, very few questions will be found in his or her speech. When this is borne in mind, our failure to find indirect standardized remarks is not surprising. Second, most of the standardized indirect questions can also be seen as a polite way to form a question. The utterance "Could you pass the salt please" is, for example, best conceived as a polite way to request the salt from someone. Polite forms of requests begin to appear around the 4th year. At this age, children start realizing that they have to use politeness markings as a way of showing their cooperation with their hearer. However, as Ervin-Tripp (1979) has found, mothers are less likely to be addressed with polite markers. Fathers and strangers are given different treatment. They receive fewer imperatives than mothers. This may be because the fathers and the strangers serve the children less often. Thus the evidence of the lack of polite forms of request in my study may well be a reflection of my focus on the interaction between young children and their mothers rather than an unambiguous indication of the child's cognitive and linguistic limitations.

The level of standardized indirectness in the mother's speech is more or less constant across the four age groups. There is no evidence of queclaratives. There is some evidence of impositives and *wh-* imperatives, but relative to all the questions that mothers address to their children, the number of the *wh-* imperatives and impositives is small. As reflected here, indirect and more polite forms of requesting are not characteristic of interlocutors who are familiar with each other. Imperatives and other direct forms occur whenever cooperation can be assumed. Conversely, the special markings we call polite are called into play whenever cooperation cannot be assumed, either because the other is considered an outsider or because he or she is less familiar with an already established pattern of communication.

Turning to the level of pragmatic indirectness in the mother's speech, there is evidence of a slight increase with the child's age. The actual numbers of this type of indirectness are so small, however, that they allow for no further comment.

The results on hinting are worth considering. First, hinting gradually increases with age. In the first age group, there are four instances of such indirectness. In the last age group, there are 21 instances. Secondly, it is interesting that, although young children score very low on the other categories of indirectness, they do produce hinting, the form of indirect speech which is considered the most complicated. In order to have their intention recognized, hints typically require a logical inference on the part of the hearer. It has been argued that the most important limit that the young child has in producing or comprehending hints is cognitive or inferential; he or she cannot do the work of drawing the inference about the desired object or act.

How, then, is the presence of hinting in our young children's speech to be explained? To answer this question, let us examine the hints produced by children belonging to the first two age groups. Most of these were of the nature "I am tired" rather than "Let's stop playing," or "This alligator" rather than "You cannot go there." For example, the child's utterance, "This alligator," received the following response from the mother: "Oh no, I will be eaten." Thus the mother perceived her child's naming behavior as an indirect remark directed to restrain her from making any particular kind of move. But can we be sure that children hint deliberately? Do they consciously restrain themselves from doing otherwise? Restraint in mentioning what is wanted is used by adults both to leave the choice to the hearer (as a form of deference) and to allude to shared knowledge under conditions of solidarity and humour. Yet it is easy to see that young children are likely to refer to the beginning stages or preconditions of need simply out of failure to specify what is wanted – as when they say "I am tired" rather than "Let's stop playing." Being nurturant, adults then complete the work for them. Similarly, given that young children spend most of their time in labeling objects around them, we cannot be sure that the choice of the child to utter "This alligator" was an active choice resulting from the proper identification of what he wanted to imply. It seems, therefore, equally appropriate to argue that the $3\frac{1}{2}$- and 4-year-olds' speech to adults often focuses on obstacles rather than on specifying their means. Consequently, although their utterances may look indirect, they appear so because they fail to be direct and are merely elliptical. Ervin-Tripp (1979) has commented on the nature of young children's indirect speech when they talk to adults. As she argues, the children's utterances may "look" indirect without having a clear intention to be so. That is because 3-year-olds often focus their attention on obstacles rather than on specifying their means when they speak to adults. Thus, although they are simply elliptical, their utterances look indirect. In the present study, the elliptical nature of the young child's indirectness was evident.

After age $4\frac{1}{2}$, there is clear evidence of hinting. Two instances of hinting were observed in the children's speech in the second age group. Both were more sophisticated than the ones produced by the children in the first age group. However, the ability to hint among children in the second age group was quite limited. Although we found a complete structural masking of the directive intent, in both cases the desired object was mentioned. The two hinting instances of the second age group were the following:

(1) "Mom don't you have a blue?" (Implying "It's your turn and you move to blue.")

(2) "I didn't have any candies." (Implying "Let me have some.")

In the two oldest age groups, the children's hinting was of a more complex nature. All of their hints were subtle and the desired objects were not mentioned. When the child hinted, both the mother and the observer were sure that he or she did so consciously and the concealment of his or her needs was deliberate. For example, a 6;8-year-old child produced the utterance, "This is a blue square, mommy!", when his mother moved there after rolling a red. There was no doubt in the mother's and the observer's mind that the child chose an indirect act to correct the mother's behavior. This was judged to be milder than simply complaining about the mother's error.

Overall, the above analysis suggests that indirectness increases with age. This offers support to Ervin-Tripp's claim (1977a, 1979) that children's language use progresses from the ability to produce and comprehend direct comments to the ability to produce and comprehend indirect or non-literal comments. This said, the research also gave rise to important questions regarding the conceptual framework guiding research on indirect speech.

Instances of non-literality in both the mothers' and the children's speech are very few. This is true for all the age groups (see table 5.6 for raw data and percentages). The most frequent subcategory of non-literality is that of metaphoric language. This finding can be explained by addressing the characteristics of language which accompanies a game interaction. All the instances of metaphor use were of only one kind, that of allocating roles in the game (e.g. "I am the pig," "You are the cow"). In the last age group, there was an increase of non-literal expressions in the mother's speech. However, when this increase was examined in detail, it was found to be primarily the result of the speech activity of one mother. She used a lot of under- and overextensions and was responsible for most of the sarcasm. Overall the instances of non-literal speech were so few that little can be said regarding this aspect of the mother–child conversations.

Comment on the indirect speech-act thesis

My review of the various cases of both the mothers' and the older children's indirectness gave rise to certain doubts regarding my preliminary definition of indirectness, a definition drawn from the philosophical literature. The indirect speech-act thesis (Searle, 1975, 1976) views indirect acts as performing two functions, direct and indirect. Unlike direct acts, indirect acts can be contextualized so as to yield two interpretations – the literal and the non-literal interpretation. However apparently sensible this distinction appears to be, my own experience suggests that problems arise when it is used to guide empirical research. To begin with, many of the indirect acts observed in the present study were conventional and standardized. Embedded in a particular context, the indirect reading of such acts, even when it has an indirect function, can be contextualized to yield no more than a literal interpretation. If, then, some formula, like "please" in (1) and (2) below, no longer admits of two readings, there is no longer any point in calling the speech act "indirect."

> (1) Can you keep playing, please? (child 6;9)
> (2) Can you please give me the dice? (mother to her 7-year-old child)

One can argue that conventional indirect acts are a special case of indirectness and that the concept is still a useful one, especially in understanding the role of "hints" in social interactions. "Hinting" can never be so strong as to force the indirect speech-act reading. However, a careful review of the instances of hinting by my subjects indicates that in some cases where hints were embedded in a particular context the indirect reading was the only one possible. For example, consider the utterance (1) "No, not the BLUE!" (child 6;6) made when the mother is just about to move into a blue square and the utterance (2) "You have a red" (child 6;7) made when the mother, after rolling the dice, looks around trying to decide where to go. Because they can be interpreted as statements and as directives, both seem indirect. However, there is an important difference between them. When the social context is taken into account, the first is unambiguously a directive. The child utters it by suddenly leaning forward, turning to the mother and waving his hand. The sudden shift in body attitude and the loud excited voice signal an urgent warning, and the intonation that accompanies the act leaves the mother no room other than to interpret it as a clear directive. This is not the case with utterance (2). Here the mother has options. She may wish to interpret it as a directive and respond appropriately. Alternatively, she might decide that the utterance is a statement and proceed in this vein.

The above distinctions are very important for clarifying the speech-acts thesis. The videotape analysis demonstrated that understanding starts from context. Thus in many situations the calculation of the speaker's intent (as this has been conceived by linguistic philosophers) is unnecessary. When a listener is attending to ongoing action and its trajectory, it is possible to understand a congruent utterance with minimal interpretative work. What is said is often redundant or adds only certain specifications (e.g. as in "please"). In such cases, alternative interpretations, including literal ones, are unlikely to be considered at all unless the utterance is so unconventional as to require an inference to reach a relevant interpretation.[2]

This discussion raises serious doubts about the usefulness of the traditional models concerning speech-act interpretation and the usefulness of the concept of indirectness in developmental research. If this term is unclear and does not seem to have a unique point of reference, what does it contribute? I believe that the concept does have a distinct point of reference, but this needs clarification. In my analysis of conversations, I found many instances of speech which were ambiguous and required certain inferences to be disambiguated. Intended meanings were often calculated from context and connected with certain general conversational principles, such as that of cooperation. However, the term "indirect" is too broad. Several distinctions need to be made among the different forms which indirectness may take. Reviewing the transcripts, I found the following distinctions to be most informative:

(1) The intonation (or non-verbal behavior) of some conventional phrases *forces* a reading which is indirect with respect to the speech-act. Without the special intonation and the conventional phrase, the whole speech-act is no longer indirect.

(2) Indirect meanings may be understood immediately (short-circuited implicatures). The interpretative process that occurs here relies heavily on context and appears to depend on expectations based on repetitions, knowledge of usual sequences, and roles. The process of comprehension here is automatic. The hearer does not have to go through the same inferential process required by a more complicated form of indirectness. Therefore he or she does not first process the literal interpretation of what is said, then check the context, identifying the speaker's intention and finally proceed with an alternative interpretation. Instead, he or she relies on his or her knowledge of what particular situations require and interprets the utterance in light of certain relevant conventions. It is only when incongruity is detected that he or she is moved to analyze the speaker's intentions.[3] In development terms, such indirect speech-acts might be easier for children to comprehend since they depend on knowledge about routines and social events. From a very early age, children have a rich system of alternations in a form that is systematically related to social features. They sensitively identify social contrasts signaled by tag modals, polite forms and address

terms. They also have learned to respond to standardized indirectness (e.g. "Could you give me the book?").

(3) Indirect meanings may also be computed. Here the meanings are
elliptical and the hearer is responsible for drawing the inference
about the desired act or object. Children by the age of 6 or 7 are
able to cope with this kind of inference and they incorporate it in
their everyday exchanges as ellipsis, as joking, or as the redund-
ancy that instructs participants about conventions.

(4) For the purposes of observational or experimental work with
children, a distinction must be made between deliberate indirectness and indirectness due to the child's inability to specify his or
her wants. To test the likelihood that young children actively hint
when they could do otherwise, it is necessary to look solely at
situations where it is certain that they know how to identify what
they want.

The development of cooperation in children's conversation

A third aim of the research was to examine how the child learns to
cooperate and how he or she becomes a better conversationalist. Here the
interest was in how and when the child produces coherent and appropriate
discourse. The focus was on two critical dimensions of the production of
this kind of discourse – "relevancy" and "speech adaptability." The first
implies that the contributions a speaker makes should be relevant to the
topic at hand. The second suggests that these contributions should be
adapted to the listener's perspective and knowledge. The analysis of the
cooperativeness of the child's speech was made in these terms.

Piaget (1959) suggested that even children as old as 5 and 6 are reluctant
to attend to one another's utterances. For the most part, children talk
alongside one another but not with one another. The child's "egocentrism"
prevents him or her both from adapting or addressing his or her speech to a
listener and from adopting the perspective of his or her interactional
partner. Insofar as the child's utterances are not contingent on the listener's
showing signs of understanding, he or she does not expect the listener to
respond appropriately. It seems, therefore, that the egocentric child is
unable to consider seriously the conversational contributions of others.
Thus children, in interacting with others, produce collective monologues
rather than dialogues.

However, overall my analysis of the child's assertions and responses
yields results which contradict the Piagetian paradigm and is consistent
with other work which suggests that children's pragmatic understanding of

language is far better than the one which surfaces in their speech (Keenan and Klein, 1975; Dore, 1979; Ervin-Tripp, 1979; McTear, 1985). I found that even $4\frac{1}{2}$-year-old children frequently made the continuation of their utterances contingent on the addressee responding appropriately. It was also the case that, as speakers, the children would often adapt their utterances to the form or content of the previous speaker's utterance. In this light, I feel that the capacity of young children to engage in dialogues has been underestimated and that the properties of these interactions deserve further elaboration.

Degree of adaptability in children's assertions

All the assertions produced by the children were categorized according to whether they were cooperative or uncooperative, and if cooperative, whether they were successful or unsuccessful. Successful assertions were primarily assessed for their degree of clarity. Moreover, most "uncooperative" assertions consisted of assertions of active opposition or withdrawal. Table 5.8 presents the raw numbers and percentages of the different kinds of assertions and responses performed by the children in the four age groups, showing that with an increase in age there is an increase in cooperative and successful assertions and a decrease of uncooperative or unsuccessful assertions.

Table 5.9 represents proportions and frequencies of the verbal or non-verbal means employed by the children for making their assertions successful. Here again we have a decrease of non-verbal dependence with an increase of age. However, the decrease is not significant.

Several analyses of variance were performed in order to further explore the children's use of assertions. Because the amount of successful and unsuccessful production of assertions could be confounded with the amount of talk, a one-way analysis was done using the percentages of the children's speech rather than the raw data. An angular transformation of the percentages was conducted in order to facilitate the statistical analysis. A highly significant difference ($F = 18.9$, $p < 0.05$) in the production of successful assertions was found among the four age groups. As children get older, they become better in producing speech which fits the listener's perspective. A highly significant difference ($F = 16.21$, $p < 0.05$) in the production of unsuccessful assertions was also found. In other words, young children often produce assertions which are directed to the listener, but the listener is not in a position to comprehend them. The difference between the age groups in the production of uncooperative assertions was found not to be significant. This finding is hardly surprising. By the age of

Table 5.8. *Proportions and frequencies of children's assertive remarks*

	Cooperative		Uncooperative
	Successful	Unsuccessful	
Age group 1 (3;6–4;0)	102 (73.4%)	22 (15.8%)	15 (10.8%)
Age group 2 (4;6–5;0)	153 (80.9%)	30 (15.8%)	6 (3.2%)
Age group 3 (5;6–6;0)	136 (96.4%)	5 (3.5%)	—
Age group 4 (6;6–7;0)	180 (100.0%)	—	—

Table 5.9. *Proportions and frequencies of verbal and non-verbal means for successful communication of assertive remarks*

	Verbal	Non-verbal
Age group 1 (3;6–4;0)	109 (78.4%)	30 (21.6%)
Age group 2 (4;6–5;0)	185 (97.9%)	4 (2.1%)
Age group 3 (5;6–6;0)	187 (98.4%)	3 (1.6%)
Age group 4 (6;6–7;0)	180 (100.0%)	— (0.0%)

$3\frac{1}{2}$, children already have a clear desire to engage in communication with adults and they do so by attempting to cooperate with them.

Overall, therefore, the results of the analysis of the children's assertions showed that even the youngest children were not bad conversationalists. About 73% of the time, children of $3\frac{1}{2}$ and 4 years of age produced successful assertions, that is assertions which the listener was in a position to understand. All our children were engaged in conversations rather than in monologues and all tried to fit their utterances to the social context of discourse.

In this context, it must be noted that young children had some difficulties. Three points illustrate the child's initial difficulties and subsequent development in appreciating the hearer's needs. First, there is a gradual improvement of successful speech with age. I found a highly significant difference between the age groups in the children's production of successful assertions. As children get older, they become increasingly better in producing speech which is in accordance with the listener's perspective and the social context of discourse. By the 7th year, all assertions produced by the children were cooperative and successful. In contrast, young children produced some assertions which were either uncooperative (i.e. personal) or seemed to be directed to the listener, but the listener was not in a position to understand them. Although the number of uncooperative assertions is substantially reduced in the second age group, there is still an equal amount of unsuccessful speech (it represents 15.8% of all the assertions produced). It is only in the third age group that there is evidence of a significant decrease of instances of unsuccessful speech.

Most cases of unsuccessful speech were unambiguous. The child was clearly directing a comment to the mother, but the mother was not in a position to understand it. This was judged to be the case by both the mother herself and the experimenter. Examples 5 and 6 illustrate some cases of unsuccessful speech:

Example 5 (1) Child (4;6): Mommy I go there.
(2) Mother: Where?
. (3) Child: Here, you see? (places cow on board)

Example 6 (1) Mother: Oh look at this one! (points at alligator)
(2) Child (3;8): Up and down mommy.
(3) Mother: What honey?
(4) Child: There (looks at board).
(5) Mother: Ok, look what I've got here! (takes toy pig, shows it to child)

Second, the data indicate that as children get older, mothers have a greater tendency to disambiguate ambiguous speech. As example 6 above shows, the mother made one attempt to clarify the young child's intention (utterance 3). But when the child failed to pick up the clarification request, the mother did not insist on it. Instead, she changed the topic by initiating a new one (utterance 5). This behavior was typical of all the mothers of the first age group. They either ignored the children's unsuccessful assertions (as if they were not potential conversational threats) or tried only once to disambiguate the child's messages. When they were not successful, they continued their conversations as if the child had added nothing. In contrast, mothers conversing with $4\frac{1}{2}$-year-old and 5-year-old children were more concerned with understanding their child's intentions than with continuing the conversational flow. In example 5 above the child is able to understand the mother's clarification request and to respond appropriately to it. I found, however, that children at this age had difficulty responding appropriately to an implicit verbal request for additional help. This is in agreement with Peterson *et al.* (1972). They claimed that 4- to 7-year-old children reformulated their messages when they were explicitly asked to do so. It was only the 7-year-olds, however, that responded appropriately to an implicit request for help. Example 7 illustrates this point:

> Example 7 Child (4;9): (shows dice to mother)
> You go there (points at dice) and then there (points at board).
>
> Mother: (looks at board, then at child)
> I don't understand.
> (pause)
>
> Child: (looks at board)
> Mother: You mean you throw this? (shows dice to child)
> Child: YES! And if you have RED you go he::re (points at square on board).
> Mother: (turns, looks at child) Ok!

It seems that the child was willing to explain his first assertive remark, but the utterance "I don't understand" did not make the problem clear. When the mother attempted to clarify her general statement, the child was able to provide additional remarks.

Third, the research revealed interesting differences in the nature of the actual conversational context in which children at different ages can engage. Although the youngest children produced assertions which were successful 73% of the time, it is important to note that the context of their interaction was very concrete and immediate. Most of the assertions produced by these children were either statements about observable objects (see example 8) or statements about simple wants (see example 9). Most children used a lot of non-verbal signs (e.g. "reaching" and "pointing") to illustrate what they could not convey verbally.

> Example 8 Child (3;9): I want this (reaches, takes cow).
> Mother: Ok, you will be the cow.

> Example 9 Child (3;8): Oh, candies! (points at candies on board)

It seems that it is in fact quite difficult to produce unsuccessful speech when the actual context of interaction is so immediate and concrete. The high frequency of adults' concrete questioning and the prevalence of immediacy suggests that 4-year-olds are not very competent as conversationalists and that therefore they (and their adult partners) adopt a strategy which minimizes the chances of unsuccessful communication. It is not that young children often talk in a way which takes the perspective of the listener into consideration, but rather that the complicated talk which requires such a consideration is rarely used. This, however, is not true of the child's conversations at $5\frac{1}{2}$ and 7 years. Their conversations are abstract, involve reference to future and past events and communicate subtle subjective feelings.

Degree of appropriateness and relevance of the children's responses

As in the case of their assertions, all the children's responsive remarks were categorized according to whether they were cooperative or uncooperative, and if cooperative, whether they were successful or unsuccessful. Different criteria, however, were used for determining successful responses. Whereas successful assertions were primarily defined by their degree of clarity, successful responses were defined by their degree of relevance. Thus responses were coded as successful if they were directly or indirectly relevant verbal or non-verbal responses. Responses which were irrelevant or uncooperative and failures to respond were coded as unsuccessful.

Table 5.10 presents the numbers and percentages of the different kinds of responses given by the children in the four age groups. Verbal and non-verbal responsive remarks are presented in table 5.11. As evidenced in these tables, we see development in the children's responses similar to that observed in the case of their assertions. There is an increase of cooperative and successful responses with an increase of age, and a decrease in the dependence on non-verbal means of communication with an increase of age.

Several one-way analyses of variance were performed to analyze the degree of successful and unsuccessful assertive responses. The statistical analysis was conducted on an angular transformation of the percentage scores for each category. The results yield an interesting picture. First, non-significant differences ($F = 2.32$, $p < 0.05$) were found in the number of unsuccessful (i.e. irrelevant) responses across the four age groups. This finding suggests that even when young children choose to reply to the questions addressed to them, they are able to place their responses in the appropriate context and do so in a manner that ensures successful communication.

Despite this ability, significant differences were found in the number of uncooperative (i.e. no responses) and cooperative (i.e. directly relevant,

Table 5.10. *Proportions and frequencies of children's responsive remarks*

| | Cooperative | | Uncooperative |
	Successful	Unsuccessful	
Age group 1 (3;6–4;0)	80 (57.1%)	3 (2.1%)	57 (40.7%)
Age group 2 (4;6–5;0)	153 (76.7%)	11 (5.5%)	37 (18.4%)
Age group 3 (5;6–6;0)	123 (90.4%)	1 (0.7%)	12 (8.8%)
Age group 4 (6;6–7;0)	97 (98.0%)	—	2 (2.0%)

Table 5.11. *Proportions and frequencies of verbal and non-verbal means for successful communication of responsive remarks*

	Verbal	Non-verbal
Age group 1 (3;6–4;0)	74 (52.8%)	66 (47.2%)
Age group 2 (4;6–5;0)	138 (68.6%)	63 (31.4%)
Age group 3 (5;6–6;0)	89 (65.4%)	47 (34.5%)
Age group 4 (6;6–7;0)	89 (89.9%)	10 (10.1%)

indirectly relevant and non-verbal) responses across the four age groups ($F=22.01$, $p<0.05$ and $F=29.15$, $p<0.05$ respectively). In particular, I found that children in the age range of $3\frac{1}{2}$ to 4 failed to respond to the questions address to them 40.7% of the time. This appears inconsistent with Stefferson's (1978) finding that 2-year-old children generally responded to questions, but their responses were often inappropriate. I did not find evidence of the child operating with the rule "If there is a question give an answer even if you don't understand it." It seems that children older than 2 years are in a position to understand rules of appropriateness and are thus less willing to violate them. However, the high percentage of the youngest children's unanswered questions leads me to agree with Dore's (1977b) claim that, for these children, failure to respond does not appear to violate a social obligation. Obviously, the ability to respond interacts with the development of the comprehension of the question.

The ability to respond to *wh-* questions develops between the ages of 1 and 6 years (Ervin-Tripp, 1970). Children first learn to respond to *where* and *what* questions and later to *why, how* and *when* questions. This sequence can be explained partly by appealing to the notion of conceptual complexity (for example, location is acquired earlier than concepts such as causality), but also by the type of response which the question requires. For example, *where* questions can often be answered non-verbally, whereas *when, how* and *why* questions generally require a verbal response. There seems, however, to be good reason to distinguish between the child's responses which are the result of comprehension of the question and the responses which reflect a realization that questions impose a social obligation to respond. There is no way of being certain that children process unanswered questions, but at least there is some behavioral evidence that they attend to most of them. Looking at the videotapes, I found that more than 90% of the *wh-* questions seemed to be deliberately not answered by children in the first two age groups. If the first decision an addressee must make after grammatically processing a question is whether or not to answer, then no answer seems to be a viable alternative for young children, and one which does not appear to violate a social obligation. The second decision an addressee must make is exactly how to answer. With age, there is a gradual increase in the proportion of answered questions. With the second age group there is, for the first time, evidence of a child's ability to go back to the question and request additional help when he does not know exactly how to answer the question (see example 10).

> Example 10 Mother:　How do you want to play it?
> Child (4;9): What?
> Mother:　Do you want to play this game?
> Child:　Yeaaaaah!
> Mother:　Ok, we have to make up some rules.
> Child:　Me?
> Mother:　No, we'll make them together.

By the age of 7, the children responded to 98% of the questions addressed to them and all of the answers were successful (i.e. appropriate and relevant).

There are also other developments that take place in the child's responses between the ages of $3\frac{1}{2}$ and 7. These have to do with the ways in which responses are used to construct coherent sequences of dialogue. The main development is in the child's ability to structure his or her conversation. In the earliest age group, I found that children could respond to simple topics (as already mentioned, these responses were usually one-word responses). Their exchanges were usually fairly closed and did not combine into larger topically and interactionally related sequences. As a result, their conversations often came to a dead end and there was a continual need for the mother to initiate new topics. Example 11 illustrates an interactional sequence of a 3;8-year-old child with his mother.

Example 11 Mother: What is that? (shows object to child)
Child (3;8): Pig.
Mother: What shall we do with that little pig?
Child: (raises shoulders)
Mother: Shall we use it in our game?
Child: Yes.
Mother: Ok, do you want to be the pig?
Child: (nods head)
Mother: Ok, and I'll be the cow.
Child: Alligator (points at alligator on board).
Mother: Yes, an alligator! Scary!!
(pause)
Mother: And what is that Justin? (points)
Child: Lion.
Mother: Good boy, and this? (points)
Child: Snake.

In the above interactional sequence, there is little or no evidence of an attempt to relate one sequence to another. For most of the conversation of this age group, each turn was independent of the preceding one. Very few instances of cohesive devices were observed. One aspect of conversational competence consists of the ability to structure longer sequences of dialogue. The major step in the development of this ability comes when children learn to set up expectations or provide for the possibility of a further response. This can be combined with the acquisition of devices for fitting more than one utterance into a turn. The result is longer interactional sequences which contain many instances of "anaphoric" reference, conjunctions (e.g. "and," "then," "well") and tags. Example 12 illustrates the interactive sequence between a 6;8-year-old child and his mother.

Example 12 Mother: Ok, here, is this a pig? (looks at pig)
Child (6;8): Yes, you will be the pig and I'll be the cow.
Mother: Ok, and then what?
Child: Well, then you take this (shows dice) and you throw it, ok?
Mother: Ok, and then I move to the right color?

Child:	Right, if it's red you go to red (points at board) and if it's blue you go there, Ok? (turns, looks at mother)
Mother:	Oh, ok!

Note how the child's remarks respond to the mother's questions. At the same time, they contribute extra commentary which both secures thematic continuity and initiates further conversation. It seems that both participants are engaging in a cooperative activity in which they seek to increment the commonly accepted set of propositions by contributing further propositions which are relevant to it. One speaker puts up some propositional information ("Yes, you will be the pig and I'll be the cow") as a relevant contribution to the topic at hand. The listener then goes on to accept it ("Ok") and contributes additional remarks ("then what?"). The first speaker then adds a further contribution ("Well, then you take this and you throw it") subject to the same constraints of relevance. Given the nature of such exchanges, cohesive devices and anaphoric references are needed to connect utterances together. The use of "it" in the following exchange determines that the word "color" has been accepted by the interlocutors as part of the common pool of shared information.

> Example 13 Mother: Ok, and then I move to the right color?
> Child: Right, if it's red you go to red.

Thus the latter proposition becomes relevant by virtue of its place relative to the set of propositions which form the common ground of the discourse.

How about the children's responses in the middle two age groups? As we have seen, the child's uncooperativeness decreases with age. However, in the second age group, there is an increase of unsuccessful responses. Although this increase is not significant, I nevertheless examined the nature of the children's unsuccessful responses. Most of these were responses to *why* and *how* questions (see example 14).

> Example 14 Mother: Why did you go there?
> Child (4;7): An alligator (points at alligator on board).

It seems that the style of the mothers' questioning of children of this age group differs from that of the style used with younger children. When interacting with the $3\frac{1}{2}$-year-old and 4-year-old children, most of the mothers do not use *why* and *how* questions. They are considered more complex than naming questions and yes–no questions. However, in interacting with $4\frac{1}{2}$- and 5-year-old children, mothers start employing complex questions. It might be the case that such questions are not easy for the children of this age group and they therefore fail to answer.

The conversational sequences of the 4½-year-old and 5-year-old children were long and coherent. However, I observed evidence of several strategies which are not present in the older children's conversations, all of which aim at achieving a coherent and sustained dialogue. One strategy children used to achieve this end was to rely heavily on the form of the mother's utterance and repeat it (see example 15).

> Example 15 Mother: Where does that go?
> Child (4;7): That go, that go (looks around board; turns, looks at mother). Where?

The second strategy children used was to rely on the mother's form of utterance and modify it slightly (see examples 16 and 17).

> Example 16 Mother: Can you go there Angie?
> Child (4;9): You can go there, ok!
> Mother: Ok, but I thought you will be eaten there!
> Child: You will be eaten there?
> Mother: Yes, that's what we agreed.
> Child: Oh, ok!

> Example 17 Mother: Well, you see we have to decide that.
> Child (5;4): You see, we have to go there (points at end point on board).

This strategy brings out the importance of separating the child's "willingness" to cooperate in talk from his or her "skill." It is clear from the above examples that despite the child's inability to maintain referential talk exchanges for longer conversational sequences, he or she is willing to interact verbally. At this level, the discourse coherence is achieved to a large extent by tying one's utterances to the formal properties of an antecedent one.

The above does not imply that the children did not have problems in conversing. In particular, children of the second age group had difficulty engaging in conversation. In some instances, it took the mother several turns to secure the attention of the child and establish a discourse topic (see example 18).

> Example 18 Mother: What do you think we do with this? (shows dice to child)
> Child (4;6): Oh! (looks at board)
> Mother: Justin, what do you think this is? (shows dice)
> Child: (looks around)

Mother:	JUSTIN! I am talking to you!
Child:	(raises head, looks at mother)
Mother:	What is that? (shows dice)
Child:	(looks at dice, then at mother) Box, BOX!
Mother:	Yes, but what do you do with it?
Child:	(looks at dice)
	(Pause)
Mother:	What is that Justin?
Child:	(raises shoulders, looks around)
Mother:	Oh come on Justin.
Child:	(turns, looks at mother) Dice!
Mother:	Well at last!
	And what do you do with the dice?
Child:	(takes dice) Throw it (throws dice).
Mother:	and . . . (looks at child)
Child:	See, . . . blue (points at dice's side) and here blue (points at board).

After the last turn, the above conversation continues with the child naming the different colors on the board. As we can see, the mother had to push the child to converse. But, after the first couple of turns, the child was able to respond and provide additional information concerning the use of the dice.

In sum, I found that contrary to the Piagetian perspective, children's conversations with their mothers were dialogues. The children attended to the others' utterances and provided relevant responses. This is not to say that children experienced no difficulty in sustaining cooperative discourse. In the beginning, their conversations were short and the topic was exhausted in two turns. However, when the interlocutor was focusing on the very concrete and immediate context, the child succeeded in producing relevant and coherent contributions. After the 5th year of life, we observed the beginning of extended themes where topic continuity took several turns. This new accomplishment became possible because of the mother's willingness to use several turns to secure the child's attention and the strategy of repetition (phonological or semantic). Repetition was used as a successful cohesive device and it was a means of responding.[4] By the age of 7 the children had become equal conversational partners. They achieved coherence by the employment of several cohesive devices and anaphoric references.

In chapter 6 these results on language use are placed in the context of the additional data on the child's socio-cognitive development.

6 Interdependence of social cognition and communication

A key issue throughout the book has been that the child's communicative ability depends on the child's increasing understanding of the social perspective of others and the social context. To communicate successfully, the child must be able to produce and comprehend utterances with reference to their social appropriateness. The models I have applied to the study of language development, the speech-acts model and Grice's conversational model, call for new perspectives regarding the conceptual underpinnings of linguistic communication. In particular, they direct us to investigate a new kind of non-linguistic knowledge – social knowledge. On theoretical grounds I isolated several parameters of social awareness that are linked to successful linguistic communication. As I argued in chapter 3, children's ability to make inferences about other people, to understand others' perspectives as different from their own, and their ability to understand what social contexts involve, are necessary underpinnings of linguistic communication.

To investigate the extent to which general social knowledge is in fact linked to language use, I examined the performance of the same children on several tasks which measure social knowledge. Here I will first present the results of the children's performance on the socio-cognitive tasks and then discuss the social interaction with their mothers that children engaged in during the game. The chapter ends with an analysis of the interdependence of socio-cognitive development and communicative development. Both theoretical argument and empirical research is presented.

The performance on the socio-cognitive tasks

The first socio-cognitive task – the "guess my story" task – investigated the child's ability to come up with a story when faced with a set of pictures which represented connected events. Here the interest is in exploring the child's social understanding and awareness, in particular his or her ability

Table 6.1. *Children's scores on the "guess my story" task*

	Age group 1 (3;6–4;0)	Age group 2 (4;6–5;0)	Age group 3 (5;6–6;0)	Age group 4 (6;6–7;0)
Subject 1	25	45	55	70
Subject 2	55	25	70	70
Subject 3	30	55	70	70
Subject 4	25	55	55	90
Subject 5	35	45	55	100

to attribute causality and his or her social knowledge. In the latter regard, the focus is on the child's familiarity with what is relevant, with what is irrelevant and with what is the sequence of events which take place during a familiar social occasion. The detailed system of scoring is presented in chapter 4 (see p. 73).

Table 6.1 presents the scores of each subject by age group. The results illustrate that the scores on the "guess my story" task depend on age. However, the task was difficult for all the children, particularly the youngest children. One $3\frac{1}{2}$-year old child was unable to perform the task at all. Three others were able to name the objects in the pictures only after the experimenter's prodding. Only one was able to identify the objects on his own. None of the children in this age group was able either to identify a single event in individual pictures or attempt to link the pictures together. We see some developments in the children's performances in the second and third age groups. All the children in these groups understood that each picture represented a social event and that these events could be linked together to represent an integrated sequence. However, the children in the second age group were unable to come up with a whole story concerning the six pictures. Instead, they focused on description and were particularly interested in labeling the event depicted in each individual picture. They also provided the first example of an attempt to link the pictures. Two children attempted this by using connective words. Both used one such word, the word "and," to link one picture description with another (see example 1).

Example 1   Ex.:   (shows the picture with the birthday cake and the boy)
                           (pause)
           Ex.:   What is that?
           Child (4;7): A birthday cake. The boy has his birthday.

Ex.:   (points at the second picture, which shows
              presents)
Child: And birthday presents . . . and the boy opens
              them.
              (pause)
Ex.:   Yes, and then what happens?
Child: Oh a snake! (points at the snake which comes
              out of the present box)

Two of the children in the third age group and three children in the
fourth age group gave descriptive presentations of the six pictures. Their
descriptions were accurate and contained many instances of connective
articles and anaphoric references (see example 2).

Example 2   Child (5;3): This boy (points at boy figure) has his birthday
              and . . . (looks around) uh . . . he has a
              birthday cake and some presents. Well, he sits
              down and opens one . . . then here a snake
              comes out and the boy is scared. Uh . . . then
              . . . a cat eats something, what? (turns, looks at
              experimenter).
Ex.:   I think that this is the birthday cake.
Child: Ok, and then the cat is eating the cake and
              breaks the plate, and then it is night and the boy
              sleeps . . . (pause) . . . and the teddy bear sleeps.
              That's the end of the story.

In the above example we see some of the child's attempts to generate a story
for the six pictures and give a casual interpretation of the events. The linking
of the pictures is done by the employment of such language as "then," "and"
and "well." There was only one child who gave an elaborated and
imaginative story to describe the six pictures (see example 3).

Example 3   Child (6;9): (looks at the pictures) Ok, I'll start from here
              (points at the boy in bed). What's his name?
              (turns, looks at experimenter)
Ex.:   I don't know.
Child: Ok, he is David. So, one day David was very ill.
              He was at his bed, and he was very miserable.
              He falls asleep and he dreams. He dreams that
              he has his birthday and his mother has a party
              for him. Here is the birthday cake (shows
              picture of cake) and here are the presents. One
              of the presents was a bad joke. In the box there

is a snake. David did not know that and he opened the box and the snake came out. He was very cross because the snake was running after the cat that David loved. Well (looks around at pictures) . . . well . . . the cat was running away from the snake and he threw the cake down. Oh no! It was a very nice cake. Oh well! "Mommy will take care of that," David said. He then put the snake into the box again. And . . . (looks around) and . . . eh . . . that's the end of the story.

(pause)

Child: I can make up another story, Ok? (looks at experimenter)

Ex.:   Do you want to play something else?

Overall, the children found the task difficult. Although most children in the last two age groups showed some ability to make causal inferences to describe social events, they had difficulty elaborating stories which contained motivational and imaginary statements. The task is more difficult because it not only requires an understanding of social events and their sequence, but also the ability to talk about them in a sophisticated and imaginative way. We can thus say that most of our 5- and 7-year-old children were able to understand what a description of a social event should be and what the relevant sequence of the several steps of a birthday is. However, they generally were not able to produce an elaborated verbal presentation of the four pictures and so arrive at a unique story.

The second task, the "face sensitivity" task, investigated the child's ability to recognize different emotions and be sensitive to the other's emotional states. The detailed system of scoring is presented in chapter 4 (see p. 74).

Table 6.2 presents the results of the children's performance on the "face sensitivity" task. The aim of this task was not only to investigate non-verbal responses to emotional representation (like, for example, Shields' 1985 study), but also verbal expressions of what the face portrays and what emotion goes with what kind of face. Virtually all the subjects found the task easy to comprehend and had no difficulty responding. Only one child, a member of the youngest age group, seemed unable to perform the task. Here again performance increases with age. The children's performances in the first age group were inadequate in several respects. A lot of the faces selected were incorrect, the faces chosen not matching the emotions of the

Table 6.2. *Children's scores on the "face sensitivity" task*

	Age group 1 (3;6–4;0)	Age group 2 (4;6–5;0)	Age groups 3 (5;6–6;0)	Age group 4 (6;6–7;0)
Subject 1	25	65	100	100
Subject 2	50	65	70	100
Subject 3	35	80	80	90
Subject 4	50	50	90	90
Subject 5	50	65	90	—

boy in the picture. In the second age group levels of performance improved. All the children were able to identify four out of five faces and were able to come up with the right emotions to match the pictures. Most, however, made one mistake in identifying one of the sad, scared or cross faces (in two of the cases, this was a careless mistake corrected by the children themselves.) The performance of the children in the third age group improved even further. Without any experimenter intervention, one child gave correct faces and correct emotions throughout the task. Two made careless face identifications which were immediately corrected by the children. The remaining two children made no errors in identifying the faces. However, the experimenter had to intervene and direct the children's attention to the emotional aspect of the picture. In the fourth age group, all the children performed without error and selected a face and matched it to a relevant emotion without help.

Reviewing these results, several points are worth mentioning. First, children as young as $4\frac{1}{2}$ made few errors regarding the representation of emotions. Second, all the children had no problems with identifying and finding the right emotion for the pictures which portrayed a happy face. Of the remainder the sad face was identified most frequently, followed by the cross face. The most difficult face proved to be the "scared" face. However, all these were identified with roughly equivalent accuracy. In sum, pre-school children appear to be operating with a two-phase scheme of emotional representation where happiness is readily distinguished, but all the other states are not clearly differentiated. This finding is in close agreement with Shantz's (1975) review, which concludes that, by the age of 4, children are proficient at identifying situations with happy outcomes and, between 4 and 7, they become increasingly accurate at identifying situations leading to sad, fearful or angry outcomes. Looking at the results of the other age groups, we can say that the ability to identify cross or scared faces develops from the ability to identify sad faces. By the age of $5\frac{1}{2}$, children are quite good at distinguishing happy from sad and cross faces. Scared and surprised faces, however, are still problematic. It is only after the sixth year that children start making finer differentiations (e.g. identifying scared faces, which originally would have been categorized as "bad" or "sad").

To conclude, it appears that there is a developmental order to the sequence in which children become capable of differentiating between emotions. Happiness is the first emotion to be reliably distinguished and this is followed by the emotion of sadness. Then we see the development of the ability to make finer differentiations along the happy–sad continuum.

The third task investigated the child's ability to take the perspective of another (i.e. to role-take) and his or her ability to make certain perceptual inferences. The detailed system of scoring is presented in chapter 4 (see pp. 74–5).

Table 6.3 presents the children's scores on the "hiding" task. Here again the results indicate that the children's performances improve with age. Two children in the first age group were unable to respond at all. Three others hid the doll, but did so right out in the open. By $4\frac{1}{2}$ or 5 years, we see some development. All children in this age group understood the purpose of the task and what was expected of them. However, they all made errors in hiding the doll. Two children hid the doll out in the open and turned the doll's head round so that it was looking away from the seeker doll, and three children hid it under the table.

Turning the doll around so that it looks away is an interesting response. As Light (1979) points out, the child in this case confuses the "not being able to see" with the "not being seen." Several mothers mentioned similar instances when playing hide and seek with their children. For example, one mother said that her child often went away and hid his face in the sofa cushions: "He thinks that when he himself cannot see he cannot be seen by others as well." The "under the table" response was equally interesting. It is worth noting that two children in the third age group hid the doll under the table as well. Although incorrect, this response is more advanced than the others. It seems that the meaning of the word "under" itself is very powerful and makes children believe that something "under" an object is well hidden. This of course is partly true. Hiding something under a table is better than hiding it right in the middle of the room. For the seeker to find the object under a table, he/she must carry out certain actions (like bending) which might be seen as being equivalent to lifting a pillow and searching for a hidden object. Apart from the "under the table" error, no

Table 6.3. Children's scores on the "hiding" task

	Age group 1 (3;6–4;0)	Age group 2 (4;6–5;0)	Age group 3 (5;6–6;0)	Age group 4 (6;6–7;0)
Subject 1	30	30	50	80
Subject 2	30	45	50	80
Subject 3	30	25	60	80
Subject 4	30	50	60	100
Subject 5	25	45	70	70

other major errors were performed by the children in the third age group. Two children made minor errors. In both cases, the error was corrected by the children themselves. All the children in the oldest age group had no problem with the task and all performed in correct ways.

To conclude, $3\frac{1}{2}$–4-year-old children have real difficulties in taking the visual perspective of another person and responding appropriately. By 4 and 5 years of age, children still have major difficulties. However, we see the first attempts to understand what it is to hide something so that another person cannot find it. The children start by understanding that hiding something "under" an object makes it more difficult to find. They also start understanding that "not being seen" must have something to do with "not being able to see." So, in an immature way, they either attempt to close the doll's eyes or turn the doll around so that she cannot see the object. It is in the 5th year that we see real progress. Here three children performed with minor errors. At 7 years, however, we see the development of a further ability. Four children not only performed correctly, but they also were able to hide the object in a place where the seeker doll could not see it, but they could. This behavior is very advanced. The child not only understands how to hide successfully, but does so without reference to his or her own visual perspective.

Overall, our results of the socio-cognitive tasks suggest that the development of social awareness and social knowledge is not an all-or-nothing affair. Rather, it is a very gradual process which starts at around the 4th year of life. Despite making important mistakes, all the children at that age showed some elements of understanding. The process appears to be completed only by the 7th year. The oldest children performed without making any errors. Although they were the only ones to do so, I feel that to conclude that the younger children are completely "egocentric" is incorrect and fruitless. The results suggest that we ought to look closely at our transcripts and analyze both the achievements and the limitations of the younger children. In so doing, we may determine which socio-cognitive parameters are problematic and which are not for children of each age group. We may thus arrive at a developmental picture of the children's understanding of their social world, in particular we may be able to understand better the performances of children belonging to the intermediate age group.

In discussing the socio-cognitive task results, there are three general issues which I feel need mentioning. First of all, there is the issue of "egocentricity" in the child's thinking. As I have already pointed out, the children did not seem totally egocentric. At $4\frac{1}{2}$ they have some ability to understand happy faces and to appreciate the situations which generate such feelings. They are also able to understand that a particular picture represents a happening and that these individual happenings might be linked together to describe a social event. As far as their visual-perspective-taking abilities are concerned, they are still rather egocentric. Although their performances are better than those of the $3\frac{1}{2}$-year-olds (who hide things right in the open), they are not successful. But by the 5th year, the children are far more competent at role-taking and making inferences about the other's internal states. These children are able to produce good descriptions of social events, to distinguish between happy and sad, cross and scared faces, and in most cases to hide an object in places where a seeker doll could not find it. Despite these achievements, their performances did suffer some limitations. Finer distinctions between similar emotional states are not made (e.g. between the cross and scared faces), elaborated descriptions of events are not given, and their visual-perspective-taking is flawed in minor ways. Only among children of the last age group did we observe error-free role-taking and visual-perspective-taking.

In this light, I believe that the dichotomy of "egocentricity vs sociality" fails to capture the real complexities of children's responses in the intermediate groups. In this respect Flavell's (1968) developmental analysis of role-taking is helpful. He argues that there are five important things that a child must know in order to achieve a role-taking mediated end: existence, need, prediction, maintenance and application. "Existence" refers to a simple awareness that others and oneself apprehend the same object or the same event differently. "Need" consists of a "growing awareness that certain situations which do not explicitly call for role-taking activity do so implicitly; that certain situations constitute a signal to engage and utilize one's role-taking capabilities" (p. 46). Further knowledge is achieved when the child, assuming he or she knows all the foregoing, succeeds in actually carrying out the intended analysis of the other person's role attributes ("prediction"). Yet further knowledge is achieved when the child reaches an equilibrium between his or her own point of view and that of the other ("maintenance"). The last concern, "application," refers to the act of behaving "appropriately" in light of one's understanding of another's perspective and of translating this into an effective verbal message. It is because of children's inability to "apply" that our understanding of children's limitations is often incorrect. As Flavell has argued, when the child produces a poor solution to a role-taking problem, it is not obvious where the trouble lies. He or she may have been unaware of perspective differences, unaware that the present task has an implicit role-taking requirement, unable to achieve or maintain an adequate representation of the other's perspective, unable to use the information contained in his or her own representation, or some combination of these. Because there are so many alternatives which can be marshaled to account for the child's failure to produce an appropriate response, I have chosen not to concentrate on the child's failures but rather on the child's successes.

Looking once again at the results, we can see that children at different developmental ages demonstrate different role-taking abilities. As I have pointed out $3\frac{1}{2}$–4-year-old children failed to perform adequately in most of the tasks. Children aged $4\frac{1}{2}$–5, however, showed the first signs of role-taking abilities. They seemed to have grasped both the "existence" and the "need" parameters of role-taking. They understood that "what is known to me might not be known to you," that "people have internal feelings and emotions which are different from mine," and that when you hide an object from somebody else you have to hide it so that "the other does not see it whereas you can see it." Their problem seemed to lie with the "prediction" element in role-taking ability. It is because of this that we see errors like "hiding the cake under the table," or giving descriptions of events which were very concrete and did not include any complicated processing of the other person's motives and emotions. By $5\frac{1}{2}$–6 years of age, most of the role-taking problems had been solved. What most children seemed to lack was an ability to apply their inferences and social cognitions and to translate them into an effective verbal message.

In relating the above findings to the children's language functioning, one can apply the same framework and observe certain similarities. Even children in the youngest age group were communicators in the sense that they were able to understand most speech addressed to them and had clear intentions that they wished to communicate. However, their linguistic functioning was limited because they seemed unable to understand how their own intentions might be different from their mothers' intentions, and how certain situations called for the need to engage in role-taking. To overcome such cognitive limitations, these youngest children were engaged in simple conversations which only involved talking about the "here and now" environment, where both children and mothers made certain that their intentions were clear and obvious and therefore did not rely on inferential abilities.

The linguistic functioning of the intermediate age groups was far more complex. Here the children attempted to "stick their heads out" and become equal conversational partners. Nonetheless, they were still socially immature. They made mistakes because they could not actually carry out the intended analysis of the other person's role and the situation's attributes. So the 5-year-old children did adapt their language to the listener's needs but only when they were asked to do so explicitly. They did attempt to produce cooperative discourse but only when the parameters of their conversational exchanges were clearly stated for them.

After the 5th year of life, children can maintain extended conversational themes and produce relevant and appropriate responses. Although their socio-cognitive development has certain limitations, these new accomplishments become possible because of the employment of certain strategies – like the strategy of repetition – which help the child deal with the social knowledge required during conversational participation. But it takes children till their 7th year to fully understand what is involved in behaving appropriately in the sense that they can understand another's perspective and can translate this into an effective verbal message.

The second general issue is that of individual differences in performance on the socio-cognitive tasks. In Flavell's (1968) studies of role-taking, he repeatedly observed a very wide range of individual differences between children of the same age. Others (e.g. Hughes, 1975) have made the same observations. I did not, however, find a great deal of individual variation in the performance of children in the same age group. Two points must be taken into account here. First, it is important to remember that the size of each of the age groups is very small. Second, Flavell has attributed some of the individual differences to environmental variation. For example, different maternal styles, different school environments and different socialization practices may lead to individual differences in the rate of relevant skill acquisition. The group I studied was very homogeneous. All the children attended the same school, came from middle-class families and were members of a small community in California. In the analysis of individual differences in the mothers' conversational style, I did not discover a great degree of maternal variation and I speculate that the socialization practices might be equally invariant. This suggests that, although there are few individual differences in the present sample, this result has to be interpreted with caution.

The third issue is that of the comparability of a child's performances across the socio-cognitive tasks. Can we speak of role-taking and social awareness of contexts as a general skill or disposition? When reviewing studies of social cognition, Shantz (1975) concludes that despite the fact that several studies have shown unexpectedly high levels of correlation, the overall picture shows only moderate relationships among the role-taking skills. In contrast, Light (1979) found important correlations across his various role-taking and visual-perspective-taking tasks. When I correlated performances across the three tasks, I found a significant correlation between the "guess my story" task and the "face sensitivity" task and between the "guess my story" task and the "hiding" task, even when the age variable is controlled for ($t = 2.62$, $p < 0.05$ and $t = 1.7$, $p < 0.10$ respectively). The first regressional correlation is hardly surprising. Performance on the "guess my story" task depends partly on the ability to make accurate emotional inferences about the psychological states of other people. Face recognition, on the other hand, depends on the ability to know the existence of certain emotions and to recognize a representation of them. At the same time, performance on the "guess my story" task depends on the ability to conceive of a set of events and create a story which accounts for them. I also found a significant relation between this and taking the visual perspective of another person into account. However, performance on the "face sensitivity" task is not significantly correlated with performance on the "hiding" task when the effects of age are controlled for. This finding leads me to agree with Flavell's rather than with Light's argument. As Flavell (1968) has pointed out, a distinction must be made between visual-perspective-taking and perspective-taking which is concerned with the affective side of role-taking. Young children develop first the ability to role-take the emotions of another person and then the ability to role-take the other person's visual perspective. The implication of this finding for our understanding of the children's communicative competence is important. It explains why even very young children do seem to comprehend certain indirect remarks addressed to them by familiar others. Often they understand them not because they are cognitively capable of complex inferential reasoning, but because they perceive the other person's emotional state. In other words, they are able to perceive the immediacy of their mother's anger or happiness rather than the effects that this anger or happiness has on their mother's verbal remarks. The above argument is, however, a tentative one. Although the present study provides evidence in support of Flavell's argument, the evidence should be interpreted with caution. The present study cannot yield firm conclusions because, when controlling for age, the cell sizes become so small that they do not allow for meaningful statistical analysis.

Social interaction between mother and child during the game situation

Here the results from the analysis of the social interaction during the game situation are presented. In an attempt to offer greater insight into the nature of the social interaction that young children engage in with their mothers, the analysis included a consideration not only of the verbal acts that participants perform to communicate with others but also of the non-verbal acts and their relation to the verbal ones.

As I have mentioned in chapter 4, the children's social behaviors (including verbal acts, i.e. speech-acts, or non-verbal acts) were isolated and divided into two groups: positive social acts (i.e. acts which are responsible for maintaining social contact) and negative social acts (i.e. acts which threaten social contact). The number of positive and negative social acts performed by the child was then computed for each of the four age groups. The original intention was to perform the same analysis for the mothers' behavior. However, it became apparent from looking at the transcripts that mothers did not engage in negative social acts. In particular, none of the mothers engaged in non-social behaviors or acted contrary to agreed rules. In most cases they were responding to their children's behavior in an encouraging way. This finding can be explained by emphasizing the semi-experimental nature of the present design. It seems that in such a situation mothers are unlikely to produce non-social behaviors. Thus the following analysis is directed only towards the children's social interaction.

Table 6.4 presents the total numbers and percentages of the two kinds of social acts performed by children of each age group. It shows that there is a decrease of negative social acts with an increase in the child's age. As children grow older they become increasingly able to engage in meaningful social interaction and do so for longer periods of time. Thus we observe that with an increase in the child's age there is a decrease in behaviors which are potentially harmful to social exchanges. Interestingly, it is not only young children's lack of linguistic sophistication that leads to the termination of social exchanges but also their non-verbal signals. As table

Table 6.4. *Percentages of positive and negative social acts during the game interaction*

	Age group 1 (3;6–4;0)	Age group 2 (4;6–5;0)	Age group 3 (5;6–6;0)	Age group 4 (6;6–7;0)
Positive social acts				
Subject 1	121 (73%)	140 (81.4%)	228 (98.3%)	153 (99.3%)
Subject 2	113 (77.9%)	158 (80.6%)	151 (96.8%)	215 (99.1%)
Subject 3	131 (66.8%)	190 (87.5%)	192 (97%)	313 (99.3%)
Subject 4	123 (65.1%)	181 (85.8%)	143 (86.4%)	197 (100.0%)
Subject 5	106 (76.2%)	132 (76.7%)	240 (99.2%)	—
Total	594 (71.8%)	801 (82.4%)	954 (95.5%)	878 (99.4%)
Negative social acts				
Subject 1	48 (27.0%)	32 (18.6%)	4 (1.7%)	1 (0.7%)
Subject 2	32 (22.0%)	38 (19.4%)	5 (3.2%)	2 (0.9%)
Subject 3	65 (33.5%)	27 (12.5%)	6 (3.0%)	2 (0.6%)
Subject 4	64 (34.9%)	30 (14.2%)	32 (18.3%)	0 (0.0%)
Subject 5	33 (23.7%)	40 (23.3%)	2 (0.8%)	—
Total	242 (28.2%)	167 (17.6%)	49 (5.4%)	5 (0.5%)

6.4 shows, there is little variation among children within the first two age groups. In the third age group subject 4 scored an unusually high number for his negative social acts. This result increased the total number of negative social acts for this particular age group. In examining subject 4's scores, it was apparent that he seemed to be unresponsive because he chose to concentrate on a different activity or on an activity irrelevant to the one that was shared with the mother, without making it explicit. His scores, however, on the other subcategories of negative acts were smaller. Also his scores on the language parameters and the socio-cognitive parameters were not substantially different from the scores of the other four children in his age group.

Table 6.5 provides a more differentiated picture of the above social acts by looking at subcategories of each act across the four age groups. It presents some interesting results. First, within the positive acts category, we have an increase of acts illustrating shared activity (from 38.3% to 58.0%) and initiating interaction (from 17.3% to 30.9%) with an increase of age. This result illustrates an important difference in the nature of the interaction children at different ages can engage in. Young children sustain social interaction by merely responding to the adult's comments or non-verbal acts. Thus the successful maintenance of interaction depends on how

Table 6.5. *Frequencies and percentages of positive and negative social acts by age group*

Positive social acts				Negative social acts		
Initiations	Responsives	Shared activity		Waiting for initiative	Non-social behavior	Unresponsive
Age group 1 (3;6–4;0)	148 (17.3%)	136 (15.9%)	328 (38.3%)	57 (6.6%)	101 (11.8%)	87 (10.1%)
Age group 2 (4;6–5;0)	284 (32.3%)	189 (21.5%)	239 (27.2%)	46 (5.2%)	36 (4.1%)	85 (9.6%)
Age group 3 (5;6–6;0)	272 (27.3%)	89 (8.9%)	576 (57.8%)	14 (1.4%)	20 (2.0%)	26 (2.6%)
Age group 4 (6;6–7;0)	284 (30.9%)	97 (10.5%)	533 (58.0%)	1 (0.1%)	1 (0.1%)	3 (0.3%)

skillful the adult is in producing acts the child can respond to. Older children, however, are able not only to respond to the other's comments but also to initiate and control the nature of the interactions. Thus, when interacting, children are active and equal participants with adults. Once again, therefore, we come to the same conclusion we arrived at when analyzing the children's conversational comments and speech-acts – young children are unequal participants and successful social interaction depends on how skillful the participant is in directing the child's focus, whereas older children are able to create social interactions which are dyadic in nature.

The relationship between social cognition and language

Throughout the present discussion I have argued that language use and social functioning are closely intertwined. The effective use of language requires a clear understanding of both the hearer and the social context in which conversation is occurring. Therefore, important relationships must exist between the child's ability to understand others, on the one hand, and the social context and his or her ability to be communicatively competent, on the other. The remaining question to be addressed is that of whether there is statistical evidence supporting the belief in the interdependence of socio-cognitive and linguistic abilities. To answer this question, we will examine the child's language use, person perception, event knowledge, perspective-taking and social-interactional abilities.

To test statistically for the relationships between the child's conversational competence, person perception, event knowledge, perspective-taking and social-interactional abilities, the intercorrelations of these variables were computed. The results are presented in table 6.6.

All the correlation coefficients in table 6.6 are significant at the 0.05 level. However, because all the variables are also significantly related to age, several regression analyses had to be carried out to control for age. A positive and significant relationship was found between successful speech and the "hiding" task ($t = 3.37, p < 0.05$), between successful speech and the "guess my story" task ($t = 3.30, p < 0.05$) and between successful speech and the "face sensitivity" task ($t = 4.02, p < 0.05$) when the effect of age is controlled for. A positive and significant relationship between successful speech and positive social acts ($t = 4.10, p < 0.05$) and a negative and significant relation between successful speech and negative social acts ($t = 4.42, p < 0.05$) was also found. Positive social acts were also positively and significantly related to scores on the "hiding" task ($t = 2.50, p < 0.05$),

Table 6.6. *Correlation matrix*

	HTASK	GTASK	FTASK	Age	PAS	NAS	SS	USS	UCP
HTASK	1.000								
GTASK	0.764	1.000							
FTASK	0.752	0.698	1.000						
Age	0.768	0.645	0.796	1.000					
PAS	0.815	0.848	0.813	0.796	1.000				
NAS	−0.817	−0.838	−0.781	−0.776	−0.992	1.000			
SS	0.869	0.804	0.901	0.839	0.905	−0.992	1.000		
USS	−0.780	−0.755	−0.751	−0.761	−0.776	0.755	−0.835	1.000	
UCP	−0.730	−0.539	−0.793	−0.640	−0.745	0.763	−0.813	0.421	1.000

Notes: HTASK = "Hiding" task
GTASK = "Guess my story" task
FTASK = "Face sensitivity" task
PAS = Positive social acts
NAS = Negative social acts
SS = Successful speech
USS = Unsuccessful speech
UCP = Uncooperative speech

to scores on the "face sensitivity" task ($t = 2.20$, $p < 0.05$) and to scores on the "guess my story" task ($t = 4.80$, $p < 0.05$) when the effects of age are controlled for.

The results provide statistical support for the claim that conversational competence is related to central aspects of social understanding. The children's ability to produce successful speech (i.e. speech which is placed in the appropriate discourse context and is relevant to the hearer's perspective) is closely related to their ability to take the visual perspective of another person, to recognize the causal links in social events and to understand other people's inner feelings. At the same time, their ability to engage in a cooperative way in social interactions is related to their ability to perform the above social tasks and to use language successfully.

In sum, person perception, event knowledge and knowledge of the social context are all closely associated with the child's acquisition of communicative and conversational competence. This suggests that the conceptual underpinnings of language are broader than much of the existing literature would suggest. In order to manipulate socially influenced alternatives, engage in discourse, and interpret speech-acts, young children draw on their knowledge of people, sequences of events and different types of perspectives.

Finally, there is an important issue which needs to be clarified. One could easily misunderstand the present purpose and conclude that the intention was to explain language development in terms of social development and thereby to reduce language explanation to social explanation. However, as Atkinson (1982, pp. 22–3) has argued:

> It is immediately apparent that, if we view this task as that of relating theories of language development to theories of general cognitive development, it bears some resemblance to the problem of reductionism . . . Summarizing there are three necessary conditions that we must impose on reductive explanations:
> (1) Theoretical terms in the reduced theory must be systematically related to theoretical terms in the reducing theory.
> (2) Formal operations in the reduced theory must be identifiable in the reducing theory.
> (3) The relevant terms and operations must appear in the sequence of theories of general cognitive development before they appear in the sequence of theories in D [Language Development].

Here, however, I make no reductionist claims regarding language development. First, I do not do so in the sense that Atkinson proposes, for I have concentrated on only one aspect of language development –

conversational competence. My aim was to argue that because it is more social than linguistic, conversational competence can only be understood when it is placed within the framework of the child's general social functioning. This is not to suggest a solely social explanation of conversational competence, but rather to broaden the analysis so as to include the consideration of social functioning. Second, I do not wish to make any claims concerning the order of development. I have no basis for claiming that social functioning precedes language ability or vice versa. The likelihood is that development in one area will coincide with development in the other.

7 Implications and applications

The chapter begins with a brief summary of the results of my study of child language development. This includes both a discussion of the evidence and the particular advantages of the pragmatic approach I have adopted. Following this summary, there is a discussion of the ramifications of the empirical investigation for philosophical models of language. The chapter closes with an examination of how the insights provided by my research might be usefully applied in practical attempts to facilitate language learning.

Summary of findings

The study reported here examines how children learn to use language in interaction with their mother. The aim of the study was to provide new insight into the development of the child's ability to become a competent participant in conversation. It thus followed recent efforts to apply the pragmatic philosophy of language to the psychology of language development. Adopting this perspective, linguistic communication was not viewed simply in terms of the specifics of what was said, but also with regard to the part it played in the individuals' attempts to act effectively in a structured social environment. This led to a study of language which focused not so much on its semantic content or syntactic form, but rather on the various ways that language can be used in social interaction.

A key finding of the investigation was that young children are far more competent in communicating than may be apparent in their speech. All the children participating in the study had a good grasp of language and were able to use it as a tool for communicating with their mothers. Even those in the youngest age group, the $3\frac{1}{2}$–4-year-olds, were able to understand most speech addressed to them, evidenced clear intentions to communicate and, in many cases, were able to do so. In this respect, the present findings are consistent with those of a number of other studies in the field (e.g. Keenan, 1974; Ervin-Tripp, 1977a; Dore, 1979; McTear, 1985).

Despite these accomplishments, the $3\frac{1}{2}$–4-year-old children's language is limited. At this early stage, children's use of language is tied to the immediate environment. Moreover, children often fail to consider the listener's perspective adequately. Consequently, their language serves only a limited number of functions and their contributions to conversation are not fully social. However, contrary to the Piagetian claims, I found that these young children's conversations with their mother did constitute true dialogues. This said, the conversations were limited. They revolved around only the immediate context, were short and any given topic was exhausted in two or three turns. Additionally, the interaction between mother and child was dominated by the mother. She controlled, directed and maintained the conversational flow. For the children, the interaction was therefore unequal and pedagogical in nature.

Between the ages of $3\frac{1}{2}$ and 7, a gradual improvement occurs in the child's ability to use language and initiate purposive acts. By the age of $4\frac{1}{2}$–5, he or she begins to extend conversational themes such that a single topic may be maintained for four to five turns. In my investigations several strategies, such as that of repetition, were employed to achieve such a result. All of these strategies indicated the child's willingness to achieve a coherent and sustained dialogue. However, the children of this age still evidenced important language limitations. Most had difficulty engaging in conversation and establishing a discourse topic. A competent interlocutor was needed to secure the child's attention and help establish and maintain a topic.

By the age of $5\frac{1}{2}$–6, the child displays increasing competence. He or she is able to produce relevant talk and to shape his or her utterances according to the listener's needs even when these are not explicitly stated. The child is more willing and able to become a more active conversational partner and thus ask questions and direct conversational exchanges. In addition, children in this age group broaden the horizon of conversation. They produce appropriate discourse contributions which are abstract and involve references to future and past events. As a result of these advances, these children become more equal participants in conversation. Despite these achievements, children at this age still have difficulty comprehending and producing complicated speech in which the desired goal of communication is not stated directly (i.e. hints).

At the age of 7, several new developments occur. The child becomes an equal partner in communicating with his or her mother. Cooperative discourse is sustained for longer periods and coherence is achieved by the employment of several cohesive devices and anaphoric references. There is also the first evidence of language use which is non-literal or indirect. Difficulties with the use of this kind of complex speech still remain and indeed may continue to do so in some children through to adulthood.

A key claim made in the book regarding conversation is that it is only one aspect of successful social functioning. Following this, I have argued that developments in linguistic ability are necessarily linked to developments in general social abilities. To explore this claim, I isolated several dimensions of social functioning which I felt were relevant to successful participation in conversation. These included the ability to understand others and their perspective, and the ability to understand social contexts and conventions. I designed a number of socio-cognitive tasks to measure the children's abilities along these lines. The tasks included (1) a face sensitivity task, (2) a visual-perspective-taking task, and (3) a social-event-reporting task. The relationship between the children's performance on the socio-cognitive tasks and their linguistic performance during the game interaction was examined. The results suggest a strong positive correlation between the two. This was true even when age was held constant (this despite the small number of subjects in each age group).

Although the study provides clear evidence of the interdependence of language use and social functioning, I do not wish to suggest that there is a simple causal relationship between the two. The matter is more complex than that. In my view, competent language use and effective social functioning imply each other. They require the same capacities to understand and direct action in everyday social exchanges. This said, language use and social functioning are not the same thing and, while development in one area is certainly related to development in the other, which area stimulates development in the other at any given point remains to be determined. Certain linguistic developments almost certainly occur as a result of the child's expanding understanding of the social world. For example, the child's ability to recognize a hint clearly depends on his or her ability to take the other's perspective. Other linguistic developments, however, occur as a result of the child's increasing awareness of the language itself and how it may be used in social interaction. For example, the child's ability to use and understand metaphors clearly depends on his or her knowledge of the relevant linguistic conventions.

In sum, I believe that the present study contributes to the understanding of children's language development in three respects. First, it broadens the scope of our thinking about language. By applying a philosophically informed model of conversational participation to the study of child language, we have isolated those aspects of participation which are particularly problematic for young children. The results of the empirical research have revealed a rich field of inquiry for those who study language as a communicative activity, that is one involving actors attempting to realize their goals in a regulated social setting. Second, the study provides an unusually comprehensive description of the development of children's language use between the ages of $3\frac{1}{2}$ and 7. Most research on children's conversation focuses on only one aspect of language use – forms of request and following response. Here a detailed description is offered of a wide range of the linguistic functions children are able to employ. This includes a consideration of both what they are readily able to do and the strategies they employ to cope with their inadequacies. Finally, the study presented here broadens the purview of the recent empirical research on child language which does adopt a pragmatic perspective. A number of the researchers doing this work assume the interdependence of language and social functioning. None, however, has actually studied this critical relationship in any detail. Offering a careful examination of precisely this relationship, the present study takes a first step in filling this important gap.

Before concluding this brief summary, I would also like to comment on the limitations of the present study and suggest directions for further research. To begin with, a number of important aspects of children's conversational participation remain to be studied. In particular, there is a need to examine the development of conversational processes such as turn-taking and repairing and to link their development to other parameters of social functioning. For example, it is likely that the ability to produce conversational repairs depends on the ability either to anticipate a failure to communicate or to be sensitive to immediate feedback from the listener. A second limitation of the present study is its focus on only one kind of social interaction, namely that between mother and child. Future research is needed to determine the relationship between the qualities of the exchange examined here and those of child–child or child–stranger conversations. A third limitation of the present study is the very limited insight it offers into the child's use of non-literal speech-acts. Little information was acquired regarding these types of speech-acts simply because they did not occur as frequently as expected. It may be that the child simply is unable to produce such speech-acts until he or she is older. Alternatively, the observed failure could simply reflect the demand characteristics of the conversational context studied here. This question could be resolved by controlling the speech situation and manipulating it so as to create a clear demand for the production of these kinds of speech-acts. In this manner it would be possible to examine how children at various stages in their development respond to a situation in which they have to ask something of a stranger (and thus are subject to rules of politeness) or in which they have to argue an issue (and thus are subject to conventions regarding the often subtle expression of wants or desires).

In addition, there were also technical limits to the present study. An important one here is the small number of subjects actually involved. A mere 19 subjects drawn from a similar socio-economic milieu do not allow for a full statistical exploration of the data nor do they provide a strong ground for generalization. Future research should seek to examine a larger number of children from more varied backgrounds. A second technical limitation is the relative crudeness of the scoring method used to assess the children's performance on the socio-cognitive tasks. The first concern of the present study was to provide a detailed picture of the child's language use. Future research should combine this with a more careful examination of the child's social activity. The key here would be to develop a fully elaborated system for scoring social functioning during naturally occurring social interactions. A model might be the speech-act system used to guide the observation of linguistic exchange. Thus the aim would be to break down social interactions into their constituent units and to understand how each unit (action) functions to realize the aims of the actors and to maintain the exchange between them.

Implications for theorizing about language

The research presented here sheds some light on both the pragmatic philosophy of language and its application to theories of language development. An important problem which arises in the course of conducting research is that most speech-act theories do not provide an adequate basis for capturing the actual properties of natural dialogue. For example, consider the following exchange encountered in my own research:

Mother:	Linzi, why don't you go to red? (1)
Linzi (4;9):	(moves nearer to brown space. Points at red tiger) (2)
Mother:	Oh I see, you are not using the dice. (3)
Linzi:	Where is red? (4)
Mother:	You can't go to the brown space because there is a red tiger there. (5)
Linzi:	(moves to red space) (6)
Mother:	Oh, ok. (7)

In this case the researcher will have difficulty analyzing the dialogue utilizing a classic speech-act model. The problem here is that non-verbal as well as verbal acts contribute to the conversation. In addition, each act is not necessarily directly relevant to the preceding one, but more to one which occurred much earlier. For example, Linzi's utterance 4 is a response not to her mother's utterance 3, but rather to utterance 1.

While no speech-act model can give a comprehensive account of how conversation proceeds, I found Bach and Harnish's model to be particularly useful for characterizing everyday conversation. While their work is closely related to Searle's, it improves on his scheme by categorizing utterances with reference to their place in the overall communicative context. Particular attention is paid to the nature of the intentions underlying utterances and the kinds of effects they produce in the hearer. The conjunction of intentions and effects are then analyzed with reference to the general principles guiding fully social conduct, most centrally rationality and cooperation. At its core, Bach and Harnish's speech-act schema (SAS) is a detailed system of making inferences together with a branching set of pragmatic strategies or understanding communicative acts. As such, the SAS avoids a problem plaguing Searle's approach. He identifies illocutionary acts with reference to constitutive rules, but fails to specify those rules in a way which allows either for the utterance of synonymous, ambiguous and indeterminate expressions, or for the performance of illocutionary acts in an indirect or non-literal manner. Bach and Harnish's SAS is designed to deal with ambiguity, non-literality, indirection, and conventional and perlocutionary acts. It is able to do so because, unlike Searle's theory, it contains no subdivision of conditions and rule. Additionally, it does not contain any special speech-act rules to attach to syntactic items and so no obviously unsolved projection problems or psychological reality problems for those rules.

Going beyond the SAS, my analysis of speech-acts was complemented by an analysis of conversational behavior. Here the nature of the interpersonal interaction was the focus and included a consideration of both verbal and non-verbal acts. This allowed for a clear identification of the relevant utterance units, even when they did not reflect the usual concerns of speech-act theories. For example, when a mother said to a child, "David, did *you* change the rule?" and the child remained mute, the child's failure to respond was interpreted to be an affirmative non-verbal reply. Another example is provided by a mother declaring, "Jasmine, you can't go there!", and the child remaining there. The choice to remain is regarded as a purposive way of making a point. (Indeed, in this instance, the mother did give up and let the child stay in the space.) Both examples provide clear evidence for Levinson's (1981, p. 479) claim that "the relevant utterance units that can function as conversational contributions can be just about anything, including nothing."

Even with this addition, I find that there are certain aspects of pragmatic theory itself which require further clarification. In particular, the term "indirect speech-act" is too broad in a way which fails to do justice to the complex way in which context, language users, and non-verbal behavior may interact in interpersonal exchanges. For example, young children often appear to act indirectly, but closer examination makes it clear that they do not do so deliberately. A case in point is a child's claim, "I am tired," which might be taken as an indirect way to end the game. However, the remark might simply be the result of the child's concentration on his or her own physical state. Utterances such as these are probably best seen as elliptical rather than indirect in nature. With these concerns in mind, I identified in chapter 5 certain categorical distinctions which need to be made when applying the concept of indirectness to developmental research.

There is a related issue concerning the role of empathy in the communicative process. All the foregoing analysis of communication focuses on the computational or cognitive processing that is involved. In so doing, it ignores what is often regarded as an important element in communication, particularly in the communication between young children and others, that is empathetic understanding. I would argue that young children may be able to respond appropriately to indirect or conversational meanings even though they are unable to reconstruct the goals of others by drawing inferences from context or social convention. In this case, understanding is not calculated, but immediate. Of course, there will be limits to this. The child will be unable to grasp, even in an empathetic way, any emotion which extends beyond his or her cognitive reach. Thus one would not expect a 4-year-old to empathize with his or her mother's ambivalent feelings towards her work. However, we would not be surprised to find a 3-year-old responding to her mother's utterance, "For god's sake, I am getting tired," as an indirect request to stop misbehaving. In the latter case, the result is probably not due to any advanced inferential skills utilized to understand the mother's goals, but rather to the ability to empathize and thus see the mother's annoyance. In such cases, understanding stems from the powerful emotional bond that children build with their mothers from infancy onwards. Thus we would expect that upon hearing the same utterance from anybody other than her mother, the young daughter will respond only with puzzlement and will not link it to her own behavior.

Another topic which I feel deserves the attention of those who construct pragmatic theories of language is that of the relationship between pragmatics and syntax. Syntax is in fact closely related to the pragmatic use of language. For example, many of the syntactic processes called "movement rules" perform the pragmatic function of indicating how information in the clause relates to what has been talked about earlier. Examples include phrases like "by the way" which mark introductions of new topics or phrases like "anyway" which mark a return to the prior topic. A developmental account of the relationship between syntactic and pragmatic functions would be of immense value. Such an account should be able to address such questions as: What are the implications of the child's acquisition of a new linguistic form for his or her capacity to engage in discourse? Or, how does the young child's lack of syntactic knowledge affect his or her conversational participation? Despite the interest of these questions, no systematic attempt has yet been made to address them.

A final conceptual issue which also deserves greater attention is the extent to which aspects of conversational competence can be taken to be universal. In this context, the question of cross-cultural or historical variation must also be considered. It may well be that while there are some very basic and general principles which apply to any effective communication, the structure of communication (and therefore the form in which these general principles are realized) may in fact vary across cultures and history, thus limiting the kinds of communication which can take place. This kind of consideration will necessarily lead beyond a simple analysis of communication in terms of its success or failure as measured against an omnipresent if ill-defined standard to a more careful consideration of the forms which communication can take and thus the various levels at which it can occur. This in turn will require an analysis of the nature of social contexts as they relate to forms of communication and thus to the types of means communicators can employ and the kinds of inferences they can make. Interesting examples of recent efforts to construct theories which consider the relationship between social structure, modes of exchange and cognition include the recent efforts of the political psychologist Shawn Rosenberg (1988) and the social theorist Jürgen Habermas (1984, 1987).

Although we do not know to what extent conversational behavior has universal qualities, strong arguments have been made to suggest it does. Such arguments claim that conversational norms have a rational origin which delimits the range of values which these norms can assume. Adopting this position, P. Brown and Levinson (1978) have presented a detailed analysis of the phenomenon of "politeness." They argue that this phenomenon can be seen as subject to several universal principles which are used by participants to structure their verbal interaction. In particular, the strategy of the speaker's willingness to cooperate and the strategy of "keeping on good terms" with the hearer in interpreting politeness phenomena derive from universal assumptions of interacting individuals: that they are rational and that they have a "face" (i.e. wants, desires and means).

In this context, it is important to remember that there certainly are significant variations in the way in which different cultures and epochs conceptualize and justify their experience. For example, in her study of Malagasy society, Keenan (1976) found that the expectations interlocutors brought to conversation differed from those of their European counterparts. A Malagasy speaker is not as direct and informative as a European speaker and therefore a Malagasy will find a European speaker much too direct and ultimately offensive and impolite. Consequently, conversational implicature (conventionally implied meaning) will differ in these two societies. However, it would be inappropriate to infer from this that what is often regarded as a universal maxim of "Be informative" does not operate at all in a Malagasy community. As Keenan (1976, p.79) argues, "To be sure we cannot imagine that the efficient exchange of information is not required to some extent in all societies."

The challenge is to develop a comparative typology which both allows that there will be locally valid systems of language use which differ from our own and yet recognizes that all are subject to certain universal constraints. The latter reflect the assumption that there are certain features of the world and of what human beings are which place certain constraints on how people conceptualize and how they can interact with one another. Grice's analysis of conversational principles directs our attention back to these universal qualities of human activity and how they determine certain standards to which all conversation must conform. In the attempt to construct a general framework for the analysis of these universal principles of conversation, one must always remember that face-to-face communication has two dimensions which must be accounted for: its social dimension evidenced by its regulated quality, and its personal dimension reflecting the fact that there are individual actors who are operating within that structure.

Applications for language learning and instruction

Throughout, I have argued that language needs to be viewed as a communicative activity embedded in a social context. In this final section, I briefly consider the implications of this conception for language learning. Here two aspects of language learning are emphasized – its interactive context and the creative use of language. In this light suggestions are made regarding the approach which should be adopted by adults interested in facilitating the linguistic development of the child. Here we consider the concerns of parents, teachers and therapists.

Children acquire language in the course of their interaction with others. It is through using words in various appropriate social contexts that they come to know their meaning. From the beginning of their language development, the children's behavior is treated *as if* it were meaningful. Thus their behavior is selectively responded to in terms of the intentions ascribed to it, ascriptions which are made in a manner consistent with prevalent cultural interpretations and context. So guided, the children come to express and to have those intentions. In other words, by engaging in interactions with others who treat their gestures and later their vocalizations as meaningful, children do indeed "learn how to mean" (Halliday, 1975). As a result of this process, they construct and reconstruct a progressively more adult-like representation of the linguistic system that provides the culturally appropriate means for their communication.

Conceptualizing language learning in these interactive terms directs our attention to the most critical and dynamic form of language use, namely conversation. Most language learning occurs in conversation at home, well before children go to school. Rather than being a precise transfer of information from one party to another, this conversation is a collaborative activity in which speaker and listener provide and use linguistic and paralinguistic cues in context. This requires a great deal of interpretation and depends on assumptions of shared meaning. As utilized by both parties to a conversation, these assumptions lead to a considerable amount of implicit, and sometimes explicit, negotiation. Engaged in such an exchange, the child is not only trying to make sense of what things mean in social contexts and to achieve "intersubjectivity," but most importantly he or she is trying to do so by building on his or her version of the "shared meaning" that is established at each point and by providing the adult with continuous feedback of how his or her contribution should be interpreted.

How then can adults assist their children in their attempt to cope with the vicissitudes of conversational exchange? Given that any conversation requires each participant to modify its behavior in light of the other's needs, what adjustments will prove to be particularly helpful to young children? A general rule which should be kept in mind here is that, when conversing with a child, the adult should always assume that the child's communicative behavior is potentially meaningful. Consequently, the adult's task is to formulate a plausible interpretation of what the child is trying to communicate in the particular situation. At the same time, the adult has another task to perform. He/she must guide the process of language learning by sustaining and extending the child's communicative efforts. In conversation the performance of each task contributes to the other. At each point the adult should attempt to ensure that the meaning he/she ascribes to the child's behavior corresponds to the child's intended meaning. This can be done in several ways. Expanding upon the child's original remark or reformulating it provides a useful test of intended meaning. Similarly, by incorporating the child's prior contribution during the adult's turn helps the child both to keep track of the ongoing line of conversation and to extend the child's original meaning.

Adults can best help children to learn language by treating their conversational contributions as important and by making them equal partners in the collaborative construction of shared meaning. The latter is achieved when the adult provides clear examples of how the language is used together with positive feedback in response to the child's correct use of language to communicate his or her intentions. Wells (1986) has provided empirical evidence which suggests that children who are exposed to a greater proportion of conversations of this kind learn language more rapidly.

Apart from this emphasis on the creative and interactive use of language, perhaps the most important implication of the argument and research presented in this book is that the development of conversational competence can be facilitated in many ways which do not involve language *per se*. Social games which require the child to recognize the other's perspective and to make sense of the other's emotions are equally important. Similarly, games which present the child with different social contexts and require him or her to infer what behavior is appropriate in each also help the child acquire the social knowledge needed for successful language use. A critical element of games of both kinds is the child's active participation. To learn most effectively one must actually be allowed to play.

Turning to educational practice, the foregoing discussion leads to a number of conclusions regarding the institutional teaching of language. To begin with, it suggests that the traditional conception of teaching – one in which the teacher is seen as a dispenser of knowledge and the pupil is viewed as a passive recipient – is seriously incorrect. The critical flaw here is a failure to take into consideration the contribution of the learner. As I have argued, the child's active contribution is especially critical for the development of conversational abilities and hence for language development more generally. This criticism of the traditional view of instruction leads to a concern with how language is used in the school. The central questions which must be addressed here focus on the extent to which children are encouraged to talk in school and whether this talk is channeled in a creative way. Are children given the opportunity to present their own ideas, observations, criticisms and comments on the meaning of whatever is going on? Are attempts made to facilitate dialogues which allow the learner to grapple with different social problems through verbal means? Are efforts made to address individuals' intentions and feelings and to establish clearly what is meant within the group? Unfortunately, most educational programs do not provide children the requisite opportunities to participate in the manner needed to best foster linguistic and social development. Clearly there is a need to carefully rethink educational practice in light of the issues raised here.

The above considerations are relevant not only to parents and teachers of children whose language is progressing normally, but also to those concerned with children who are experiencing language problems. In particular, they suggest the kind of model that should be adopted both for conceptualizing the nature of language problems and for designing therapeutic interventions. Such a model should see the child as the creator of conversational meaning. It should focus less on what he or she cannot do and more on what he or she can do. In so doing, it must illuminate the nature of the strategies that a particular child has constructed to cope with his or her language problems and judge how effective these strategies are in given social situations. Therapeutic interventions must be structured accordingly. They must build on a general recognition of the interactive and social dimension of language development and a specific understanding of the communicative activity of the particular child in question. In this light, the orientation commonly adopted by language therapists, with its focus on the individual and static aspects of language, must be regarded as inadequate. McTear makes a number of appropriate suggestions as to how to take into account the interactive quality of language learning. Guided by a perspective similar to the one I have presented here, he recommends therapy be more directed towards "interaction with others such as parents and peers rather than working entirely within one-to-one therapy situations, [and should be] looking critically at the use of test questions, which usually violate rules of sincerity and naturalness and [should be] tailoring the environment to a greater extent to the patient's needs and interests, for example by encouraging and responding to the patient's initiations" (McTear, 1985, p. 255).

To design specific intervention methods or therapy programs, we first need to isolate the causes of the language problem being addressed. The present book, by emphasizing the social dimension of language, not only broadens the scope of the theory of language, but also suggests a new frame of reference within which to make sense of various language disorders and to craft appropriate clinical responses. To illustrate this, let us consider the case of language-delayed children. Some of them may have problems related to the specifically linguistic aspect of the communicative process; others, however, will have problems which are basically social. For example, some language-delayed children have phonological or syntactic problems, but no difficulty in generating specific communicative intentions and placing them in appropriate social contexts. On the other hand, other children with this language problem seem to have no vocabulary problem but have difficulty generating socially appropriate communications. As these cases suggest, our assessment methods should be diverse and should evaluate the social-interactive as well as the linguistic dimension of language disorders. Once the critical aspect of the problem has been determined, therapeutic interventions should be directed accordingly.

Many other language problems in addition to language delay may stem from specifically social problems. An interesting case in point, in part because its relation to social competence is apparently remote, is that of reading. My own work at the Neurolinguistic Clinic of the University of California, Irvine, is relevant here.[1] I have been involved in a project examining the links between children's reading problems and their conversational and social abilities. Although the project is still in its initial stages, the early findings are suggestive. For a number of the children reading problems are correlated with conversational problems. This should not be surprising if we consider for a moment what reading involves. As a reader the child confronts obstacles similar to those he or she faces as a participant in a conversation. In order to comprehend a reading passage, he or she must enter the world being constructed by the author. To do so, the child must role-take and appreciate the intentions of the author which lie behind the various events and characters presented. This also necessitates the child mastering the appropriate social knowledge to facilitate the interpretation of what is being communicated. All this is required in conversation as well as in reading, although in the case of reading these social inferential tasks are complicated by the fact that the author is absent and is therefore less able to interact with his or her audience.

Guided by this view of reading, the aims of the project are (1) to identify children who have reading problems which are connected to problems of conversation and social interaction, and (2) to design a training method which not only teaches them how to read according to traditional methods, but also teaches them to appreciate reading and language as a whole. Here the emphasis will be on helping children understand the social nature of language and its use in face-to-face or imaginary interactions. Following this, reading exercises will be designed not only to concentrate on how written words can be appropriately transformed into oral ones, but also to facilitate an understanding of the written text as a whole. This will involve a consideration of such factors as the pragmatic presuppositions entailed in communication and the social knowledge required for interpretation.

The assumptions underlying the reading project and the trajectory it is following have important ramifications for the practice of educationists and clinicians interested in the assessment of language abilities. This assessment should include an examination of the child's language functioning, that is an evaluation of his or her communicative competence. Because language use is tied to the child's total experience, and this use varies with the topic, the interactors and the setting, a multi-information approach is needed to properly evaluate language abilities and language problems. In the reading project, the assessment procedure designed thus far includes (1) a communication sample (an expressive language sample with contextual information) of the child interacting with the mother and then with the teacher; (2) a story-telling sample of the child telling a story to an adult; and (3) a standardized test of reading. The communication samples yield information on both the child's functional language use (the analysis here focuses on speech-act performance and conversational style) and the surface structure of his or her language (e.g. mean length of utterances). The retelling of a story provides information on the child's ability to store in memory a story previously told and on his or her ability to adjust the communication of this story to the needs of the listener and the context of the discourse.

Seen in this context, it is apparent that the third assessment, the standardized test of reading, yields only a partial account of the complexities of the language problems the children have. It is only when all three tests are used that we see that different children's problems stem from different sources. Some are due to failures in recognizing words or analyzing the syntax of text, others to failures to organize and store in memory the requisite concepts and social knowledge, and still others to failures to appreciate the pragmatic dimensions of discourse. Interventions designed to improve the reading of the last two groups clearly cannot follow traditional approaches. Rather, interventions in these cases should be designed so as to increase the children's social knowledge and conversational abilities.

I do not wish to imply that the separation of pragmatic problems from syntactic or phonological ones is an easy task. There are certainly instances where such a separation is readily made. For example, as McTear (1985) points out, dysphasic children seem to have more problems with syntax than with conversation. In contrast, autistic children have far more problems with conversation than with phonology and syntax. For the vast majority of language problems, however, the separation is problematic. Empirical research on children with language problems should be of great help; however, a theoretical framework is needed to elucidate the exact nature of the relationship between conversation and other aspects of language. As mentioned earlier, no systematic attempt has been made to construct a theory of how pragmatics relates to "core linguistics" (apart from semantics). This is clearly a task which must be undertaken. I do believe, however, that a careful description of the social and linguistic issues underlying communication such as the one offered here provides a promising start.

Appendix 1

Transcription conventions and transcription symbols for utterances

Units

A unit is an utterance and/or an act performed by one participant at a given time. It is bounded by a significant pause or by an utterance or an act of the other participant. Each unit is numbered separately in the sequence in which it occurred. Pauses are not precisely timed. However, significant pauses between utterances of the same participant are taken to represent a "floor change" and are recorded as a different unit with a different number. Behaviors that occurred at the same time by two different participants are marked with the same number.

Transcription symbols for utterances

Loudness	Marked by using capital letters. E.g. "Come HERE."
Emphasis	Marked by italicizing the specific word within a given utterance. E.g. "You mean you want *this*?"
Lengthened syllable	Marked by colons "::". E.g. "This is gre::en."
Intonation	"," marks low rise. "?" marks high rise. Reference to the general ongoing activity was also made in identifying questions. "." marks low fall. "!" marks exclamatory utterances.
(Utterance)	Used whenever an utterance was unclear to the observer but tentative interpretation of words or phrases was possible.

| (U) | Used whenever an utterance was uninterpretable by the observer. |
| (WH) | Whispers. |

The transcriptions of non-verbal acts were adapted from the Behavior Catalogue, compiled by Jim Chisholm, Fae Hall, Nick Blurton-Jones and Rob Woodson, April 1974.

Extracts from the videotape transcripts

Child 6;9

	Child		Mother	
Non-verbal	Verbal	Verbal	Non-verbal
1 Sits down	1 Ok! Let's play it	—	1 Sits, looks at child
2 Looks where mother points	—	2 What is	2 Points at board
3 Looks at board	3 Go,	3 this?	3 Looks at board
	4 This is the starting point.	4 Right	4 Looks at board
5 Points at pathways	5 And you can move into here		5 Looks at board
6 Raises head, looks at mother	6 into two turns		6 Looks at board
7 Looks at board		7 And how do you get turns?	7 Looks at child
8 Looks around	8 Eh, we . . .,		8 Looks at child
9 Points at dice	9 we, eh, pick a number on this!		9 Looks down at board

Child 6;8

Child		Mother	
Non-verbal	Verbal	Verbal	Non-verbal
1 Turns dice	1 You turn turn	1 You	1 Extends hand, takes dice
2 Sits	2 That's a dice		2 Glances at child
3 Watches		3 A number?	3 Looks at dice
4 Plays with feet	4 Ye::ah!		4 Looks at child
5 Looks at mother	5 Like you pick a six and		5 Looks at child
6 Looks at mother	6 I'll be two and that's		6 Nods head
7 Turns, looks	7 a number(!) number(!)		7 Looks at child
8 Sits back		8 Ok, you roll it	
9 Looks at mother		9 like that?	9 Rolls dice
10 Looks at mother	10 Yeah(!)		10 Looks at child
11 Looks at dice		11 But, I don't see any NUMBERS!	11 Looks closely at dice
12 Looks at mother	12 You can		12 Raises head
13 Looks at dice	13 make them UP		13 Looks at child

Child 4;6

Child		Mother	
Non-verbal	Verbal	Verbal	Non-verbal
1 Looks at mother		(pause)	1 Looks at board
2 Looks where mother looks		2 You know what we could	2 Looks at dice
3 Looks at mother		3 do?	3 Raises head, looks at child
4 Shakes head, looks at mother	4 What?		4 Shows dice to child
5 Looks at mother		5 We could roll the dice, and	5 Rolls dice
6 Watches mother		6 whatever color comes on top we go	6 Points at colors on dice
7 Watches mother		7 there!	7 Turns, looks at child
8 Nods head	8 Ok!		8 Smiles
9 Takes dice		9 And where are we going to?	9 Looks at board
10 Leans forward, points	10 The finishing line is here		10 Watches child

Child 5;7

Child		Mother	
Non-verbal	Verbal	Verbal	Non-verbal
1 Looks at board		1 Ok, that's what we get, because what is in there?	1 Looks at board
2 Turns, looks at candies	2 I don't know,		2 Leans forward looks closely at board
3 Turns, looks at mother	3 what that?		
4 Looks at mother		4 I think these are candies!	4 Looks at board
5 Nods head		5 Who do you want to be?	5 Makes pig stand
6 Takes pig	6 I'll be the pig		6 Looks down
7 Raises head, looks at mother	7 And you'll be the cow,		7 Takes cow
	8 ok?		8 Looks at child
9 Looks at mother		9 Ok!	9 Puts cow to starting point

Appendix 2

The relationship of utterances and speech-acts

In the present analysis two different measures have been taken for analyzing each verbal unit.

(1) Utterances

Any uttered sound which occupied a speaking turn. No attention was paid to full stops. Each utterance had finished when there was either a pause or when the speaking turn was taken by the other person.

(2) Speech-acts

A particular utterance could be coded as representing several speech-acts. For example, the utterance "Look, the boy doesn't have a head" was coded as being an assertion about an event and an attention-seeking act.

Definitions of speech-acts and their subcategories

Assertives
Any utterance which reports facts, states rules, conveys attitudes.

(a) Assertions about objects (labeling). Any one-word assertion which merely labels a perceivable object.
E.g. "Yellow," "Cow."

(b) Assertions about events. Any statement which predicates events, properties and locations, and describes objects, events and people, or states definitions of social rules.
E.g. "It fell on the floor," "That happens later."

(c) Assertions about internal phenomena. Any assertions about emotions, sensations, intentions, and any other internal events.
E.g. "I like it," "I don't know."

Responsives
Any utterance which supplies solicited information to a prior requestive act.

(a) Supplying solicited one-word information. A one-word response to a prior requestive.
E.g. "Yes," "Green."
(b) Supplying extended response. An elaborated response to a prior requestive act.
E.g. "Because it must go in here."

Requestives
Any utterance which solicits information or action.

(a) Questions (real, test, or verbal reflective). Any utterance which requests information.
E.g. "What is that?"
(b) Requests for action. Any utterance which seeks the performance of an action by the hearer.
E.g. "Go over there."
(c) Suggestions. Any utterance which recommends the performance of an action by hearer or speaker.
E.g. "Shall we do that?"

Commissives
Any utterance which looks forward and promises an offer or a claim to the hearer.

E.g. "I promise I'll do that," "When we reach this point we'll have to go back three spaces."

Expressives
Any non-propositional utterance which conveys attitudes or repeats or acknowledges others.

(a) Exclamations. Those conveying attitudes.
E.g. "Oh," "Ah."
(b) Accompaniments. Those maintaining contact by supplying information which is redundant in respect to some contextual feature.
E.g. "Here you are," "There you go."

(c) Repetitions. Those repeating own or the speaker's prior utterance.
(d) Attention-seeking devices.
E.g. "Hey John," "Look!"

Acknowledgment
Any non-propositional utterance which recognizes prior non-requestive utterances, and helps the maintenance of the conversational flow.

(a) Agreeing or rejecting prior utterances.
E.g. "Yeah," "Ok."
(b) Praising or thanking.
E.g. "Good Boy," "Thanks."
(c) Apologizing.
E.g. "Oh sorry."
(d) Greetings.
E.g. "Hello."

Personal
Any utterance which is directed to self rather than others.

E.g. "I'll put that here, and that there." The child utters this sentence without looking at the adult and while she is playing by herself.

Uncodable
Any utterance which is either uninterpretable or uncodable (i.e. does not fall in any of the above categories) to the observer at the stage of transcription.

Definitions of the categories for scoring social interactional acts

Positive behaviors

Initiations
Any verbal or non-verbal act which looks forward and requires another person to speak.

(a) Labeling. The child initiates conversation by labeling objects in the immediate environment.
E.g. "Cow."
(b) Stating. The child initiates conversation by stating extra information.
E.g. "This goes here."
(c) Requesting. The child initiates conversation by requesting information or action from his or her partner.
E.g. "What do we do now?"

(d) Non-verbal. The child initiates conversation by non-verbal means.

E.g. (takes, shows pig to mother).

Responsives
An act which supplies information to a prior requestive act.

(a) One-word. The child responds with a one-word utterance.

E.g. "Yes."

(b) Extended. The child responds with a more than one-word utterance.

E.g. "You'll be the pig."

(c) Non-verbal. The child responds by non-verbal signs.

Shared activity

(a) Watching. The child watches what his or her partner does.

E.g. Mother: "Oh, I'll go here" (moves to right color on board).

Child: (watches closely mother's actions).

(b) Giving/taking.

E.g. When the child has finished with his or her turn, he or she gives the dice to the mother for her turn.

(c) Laughing/smiling. The child laughs or smiles during a shared joke.

(d) Concentrating on relevant activity. The child's attention is directed to an activity or an object which is directly relevant to the immediate context of the interaction.

E.g. Mother throws dice and child attempts to make cow stand on the right place on board.

(e) Acts following agreed rules. The child acts in a way which takes into account the rules that have been decided.

E.g. The child at his or her turn takes and throws the dice.

Negative behaviors

Waiting for initiation

(a) Staring. The child sits and stares at game board or mother.
(b) Motionless. The child sits motionless, looks around or straight ahead, showing complete lack of interest.

Non-social behaviors

(a) Child *cries.*
(b) Child attempts *to leave the room or to terminate the game interaction.*
(c) Child *acts against agreed rules.*
(d) Child *concentrates on different activity* from his or her partner without attempting to share it with him or her.
(e) Child *talks to self.*

Unresponsiveness

(a) Child fails to respond to prior request because he or she is concentrating on a *different activity.*
(b) Child fails to respond to prior request and sits *motionless* looking at mother.

Notes

2 Toward an elaborated model of language

1 Grice's intention is to make universal claims. However, because of the considerable cultural variation in the Gricean principles (see Keenan, 1976), it seems better to see them as defining some parameters that need specification in particular cultures.

5 Evidence on language use

1 Tables A and B present the mean scores and standard deviations of the classes of conversational activity for first the children of each age group and then for their mothers.

Table A. *Distribution of the child's scores within age groups*

		Age group 1 (3;6–4;0) N = 5	Age group 2 (4;6–5;0) N = 5	Age group 3 (5;6–6;0) N = 5	Age group 4 (6;6–7;0) N = 4
Assertives	X	21.8	37.0	37.4	45.0
	SD	12.4	20.2	21.2	8.7
Responsives	X	14.8	27.6	17.8	23.7
	SD	8.5	13.2	9.9	1.7
Requestives	X	4.4	10.2	13.2	23.5
	SD	4.1	4.6	4.3	10.3
Expressives	X	2.4	7.0	7.6	10.0
	SD	1.5	2.6	5.2	4.8
Acknowledgment	X	4.0	10.6	10.6	14.0
	SD	2.9	7.0	7.6	4.5
Commissives	X	0.0	1.0	1.4	2.5
	SD	0.0	1.7	2.4	3.1
Uncodable	X	4.4	7.8	4.1	2.1
	SD	3.1	1.3	1.5	1.8
Personal	X	5.0	0.6	0.0	0.0
	SD	3.1	1.5	0.0	0.0

Table B. *Distribution of the mother's scores within age groups*

		Age group 1 (3;6–4;0) N=5	Age group 2 (4;6–5;0) N=5	Age group 3 (5;6–6;0) N=5	Age group 4 (6;6–7;0) N=4
Assertives	X	31.4	26.8	40.4	40.2
	SD	7.6	5.8	15.2	10.1
Responsives	X	1.0	2.8	3.4	9.5
	SD	0.8	2.2	1.6	3.4
Requestives	X	39.2	48.6	31.8	32.0
	SD	6.4	4.1	19.8	9.5
Expressives	X	7.4	9.8	10.0	10.0
	SD	4.1	5.6	4.0	8.4
Acknowledgment	X	13.0	27.4	13.4	17.5
	SD	5.4	13.6	2.0	8.3
Commissives	X	1.6	0.8	0.8	0.7
	SD	1.6	1.5	1.2	1.1
Uncodable	X	2.2	4.0	2.1	0.8
	SD	2.1	3.6	1.8	0.5
Personal	X	0.0	0.0	0.0	0.0
	SD	0.0	0.0	0.0	0.0

2 In the latter regard, I am in agreement with Ervin-Tripp (1979, p. 207) who writes: "We can say that interpretation is retrospective to context . . . We propose that participants become aware of inferential processes when there is incongruity or misunderstanding and that this awareness has been the model for standard interpretation."

3 A similar argument has been made by Ervin-Tripp and Gordon (1980) in their analysis of requests. They propose a contextually based model for understanding several types of requests. As they write, "there is a kind of momentum in situations which does not require a constant assessment of intention in others unless there is some clash between what the actor construes to be the larger activity goals and what is said at a particular moment" (p. 140).

4 This finding agrees with Keenan's (1977) and McTear's (1978) findings on the children's strategy of repetition.

7 Implications and applications

1 The project is being conducted with Dr Anne Kaganoff, Director of the Neurolinguistic Clinic, and with Dr Michelle Wilson, a speech pathologist.

References

Acredolo, L. (1977) Developmental changes in the ability to coordinate perspectives of a large-scale space. *Developmental Psychology*, 13: 1–8

Arwood, L. (1983) *Pragmaticism: Theory and Application*. Rockville, MD, Aspen

Atkinson, R. M. (1979) Prerequisites for reference. In E. Ochs and B. Schieffelin (eds.), *Developmental Pragmatics*. New York, Academic Press
    (1982) *Explanations in the Study of Child Language Development*. Cambridge, Cambridge University Press

Atkinson, R. M. and Drew, P. (1979) *Order in Court*. London, Macmillan

Atkinson, R. M. and Griffith, K. (1973) Here is here, there is there and here. *Edinburgh Working Papers in Linguistics*, 3: 29–73

Austin, J. L. (1962) *How to do Things with Words*. Oxford, Clarendon Press

Auwera, J. V. (1980) *Indirect Speech Acts Revisited*. Bloomington, Indiana University Linguistic Club

Bach, K. and Harnish, R. M. (1979) *Linguistic Communication and Speech Acts*. Cambridge, MA, MIT Press

Bates, E. (1976) *Language and Context: The Acquisition of Pragmatics*. New York, Academic Press

Bates, E., Benigni, L., Bretherton, I., Camaioni, L. and Volterra, V. (1977) From gesture to the first word: on cognitive and social prerequisites. In M. Lewis and L. Rosenblum (eds.), *Interaction, Conversation and the Development of Language*. New York, Wiley

Bates, E., Camaioni, L. and Volterra, V. (1979) The acquisition of performatives prior to speech. In E. Ochs and B. Schieffelin (eds.), *Developmental Pragmatics*. New York, Academic Press

Bellinger, D. (1979) Changes in the explicitness of mother's directives as children age. *Journal of Child Language*, 6: 443–58

Berlinger, G. and Garvey, C. (1981) Relevant replies to questions: answers versus evasions. *Journal of Psycholinguistic Research*, 10 (4): 403–20

Bloom, L. (1970) *Language Development: Form and Function in Emerging Grammars*. Cambridge, MA, MIT Press
    (1973) *One Word at a Time*, The Hague, Mouton

Bloom, L., Lightbown, P. and Hood, L. (1975) *Structure and Variation in Child Language*. Monographs of the Society for Research in Child Development 40, 2. Chicago, University of Chicago Press

Borke, H. (1971) Interpersonal perception of young children: egocentricism or empathy? *Developmental Psychology*, 5: 263–9
  (1973) The development of empathy in Chinese and American children between 3 and 6 years of age. *Developmental Psychology*, 9: 102–8

Bowerman, M. (1981) Cross-cultural perspectives on language development. In H. C. Triandis (ed.), *Handbook of Cross-Cultural Psychology*. Boston, Allyn and Bacon

Braine, M. D. S. (1963) The ontogeny of English phrase structure: The first phase. *Language*, 39: 1–13

Brown, P. and Levinson, S. (1978) Universals in language usage: politeness phenomena. In E. N. Goody (ed.), *Questions and Politeness: Strategies in Social Interaction*. Cambridge, Cambridge University Press

Brown, R. and Fraser, C. (1964) The acquisition of syntax. In U. Bellugi and R. Brown (eds.), *The Acquisition of Language*. Monographs of the Society for Research in Child Development, 29. Chicago, Chicago University Press

Bruner, J. (1975) The ontogenesis of speech-acts. *Journal of Child Language*, 2: 1–20
  (1978) On pre-linguistic prerequisites of speech. In R. N. Campbell and P. T. Smith (eds.), *Recent Advances in the Psychology of Language: Language Development and Mother–Child Interaction*. New York and London, Plenum Press
  (1981) The social context of language acquisition. *Language and Communication*, 1, 2/3: 155–78

Bryant, P. (1975) The development of social cognition. In E. Hetherington (ed.), *Review of Child Development Research*, vol. 5. Chicago, University of Chicago Press

Campbell, R. N. (1979) Cognitive development and child language. In P. Fletcher and M. Garman (eds.), *Language Acquisition*. Cambridge, Cambridge University Press

Carter, A. (1978) From sensori-motor vocalizations to words: a case study of the evolution of attention directing communication in the second year. In A. Lock (ed.), *Action, Gesture and Symbol: The Emergence of Language*. New York, Academic Press

Chandler, M. J. (1977) A selective review of current research. In W. F. Overton and J. M. Gallagher (eds.), *Knowledge and Development*, vol. 1. New York and London, Plenum Press

Chomsky, N. (1965) *Aspects of the Theory of Syntax*. Cambridge, MA, MIT Press.

Cicourel, A. V. (1981) The role of cognitive and linguistic concepts in understanding everyday social interactions. *Annual Review of Sociology*, 17: 42–71

Clark, E. V. (1978) Strategies of communication. *Child Development*, 49: 953–9

Clark, H. H. (1975) Understanding what is meant from what is said: a study of conversationally conveyed requests. *Journal of Verbal Learning and Verbal Behavior*, 3: 56–70

Clarke-Stewart, A. (1978) *The Development of Social Understanding*. New York, Gardner Press

Cooper, D. (1973) *Philosophy of the Nature of Language*. London, Longman

Dale, P. S. (1972) *Language Development: Structure and Function*. New York, Holt, Rinehart and Winston

Damon, W. (1977) *The Social World of the Child*. San Francisco, Jossey

De Villiers, J. C. and de Villiers, P. A. (1979) *Language Acquisition*. Cambridge, MA, Harvard University Press

Dore, J. (1975) Holophrase, speech acts and language universals. *Journal of Child Language*, 2: 21–40

(1977a) Children's illocutionary acts. In R. Freedle (ed.), *Discourse, Production and Comprehension*. Hillsdale, NJ, Lawrence Erlbaum

(1977b) On them sheriff: a pragmatic analysis of children's responses to questions. In S. Ervin-Tripp and C. Mitchell-Kernan (eds.), *Child Discourse*. New York, Academic Press

(1979) What's so conceptual about the acquisition of linguistic structures. *Journal of Child Language*, 6: 129–37

Downing, J. (1985) The child's understanding of the functions and processes of communication. In M. M. Clark (ed.), *New Directions in the Study of Reading*. New York, Falmer

Ervin-Tripp, S. (1970) Discourse agreement: how children answer questions. In J. R. Hayes (ed.), *Cognition and the Development of Language*. New York, Wiley

(1977a) Early discourse: some questions about questions. In M. Lewis and L. Rosenblum (eds.), *Interaction, Conversation and the Development of Language*. New York, Wiley

(1977b) Wait for me roller-skate! In S. Ervin-Tripp and C. Mitchell-Kernan (eds.), *Child Discourse*. New York, Academic Press

(1978a) Some features of early child–adult dialogues. *Language in Society*, 7: 357–73

(1978b) Whatever happened to communicative competence? In *Proceedings of the Linguistic Forum* (September). Champaign-Urbana, University of Illinois

(1979) Children's verbal turn-taking. In E. Ochs and B. Schieffelin (eds.), *Developmental Pragmatics*. New York, Academic Press

(1981) How to make and understand a request. In H. Parret, M. Sbisà and J. Verschueren (eds.), *Possibilities and Limitations of Pragmatics*, Proceedings of the Conference on Pragmatics, Urbino, 8–14 July 1979. Amsterdam, Benjamins

Ervin-Tripp, S. and Gordon, D. P. (1980) The development of requests. In R. E. Schiefelbusch (ed.), *Communicative Competence: Acquisition and Intervention*. Baltimore, Baltimore University Press.

Ervin-Trip, S. and Kernan, C. (1977) *Child Discourse*. New York, Academic Press

Fantz, R. D. (1965) Visual perception from birth as shown by pattern selectivity. *New York Academy of Science*, 188: 793–814

Fein, D. A. (1972) Judgement of causality to physical and social picture sequences. *Developmental Psychology*, 8: 147–65

Flavell, J. H. (1968) *The Development of Role-Taking and Communication Skills in Children*. New York and London, Wiley

    (1974) *The Development of Inferences about Others*. In T. Mischel (ed.), *Understanding Other Persons*. Oxford, Blackwell

Flavell, J. H. and Ross, L. (1981) *Social Cognitive Development: Frontiers and Possible Futures*. Cambridge, Cambridge University Press

Gardner, H., Winner, E., Bechlofer, R. and Wolf, D. (1978) The development of figurative language. In Nelson, K. E. (ed.), *Children's Language*, vol. 1. New York, Gardner

Garvey, C. (1975) Requests and responses in children's speech. *Journal of Child Language*, 2: 41–63

    (1977) Play with language and speech. In S. Ervin-Tripp and C. Kernan (eds.), *Child Discourse*. New York, Academic Press

    (1979) Contingent queries and their relations in discourse. In E. Ochs and B. Schieffelin (eds.), *Developmental Pragmatics*. New York, Academic Press

Garvey, C. and Hogan, R. (1973) Social speech and social interaction: egocentricism revisited. *Child Development*, 44: 562–8

Gibbs, R. W. (1987) Linguistic factors in children's understanding of idioms. *Journal of Child Language*, 14: 569–86

Ginsberg, E. H. (1982) Linguistic input and the child's acquisition of language. *Psychological Bulletin*, 92, 1: 3–26

Goldman, S. R. (1982) Knowledge systems for realistic goals. *Discourse Processes*, 5: 279–303

Grice, H. P. (1975) *Logic and Conversation*. In Cole, P. and Morgan, J. L. (eds.), *Syntax and Semantics*, vol. 3, *Speech-Acts*. New York, Academic Press

Gruber, J. (1967) Topicalization in child language. *Foundations of Language*, 3: 37–65

Gumperz, J. J. (1972) Introduction. In J. J. Gumperz and D. Hymes (eds.), *Directions in Socio-Linguistics: The Ethnography of Communication*. New York, Holt, Rinehart and Winston

    (1982) *Discourse Strategies*. Cambridge, Cambridge University Press

Habermas, J. (1984) *Towards a Theory of Communicative Action*, vol. 1. Boston, Beacon Press

    (1987) *Towards a Theory of Communicative Action*, vol. 2. Boston, Beacon Press

Halliday, M. A. K. (1975) *Learning How to Mean*. London, Edward Arnold

Hamlyn, D. W. (1978) *Experience and the Growth of Understanding*. London, Routledge and Kegan Paul

Hee-Seo Park, L. (1980) Sensitivity to Social Situations. Unpublished PhD. thesis, University of California, Irvine, CA

Hirst, P. (1975) Language and thought. In R. S. Peters (ed.), *Education and the Development of Reason*. London, Boston and Henley, Routledge and Kegan Paul

Howe, C. J. (1978) *Acquiring Language in a Conversational Context*. New York, Academic Press

(1983) Concepts and methods in the study of conversation: a reply to L. Olsen-Fulero. *Journal of Child Language*, 10: 231–7

Hughes, M. (1975) Egocentricism in Pre-school Children. Unpublished doctoral dissertation, University of Edinburgh

Huttenlocher, J. and Presson, C. (1973) Mental rotation and the perspective problem. *Cognitive Psychology*, 4: 277–99

Hymes, D. (1971) Competence and performance in linguistic theory. In R. Huxley and E. Ingram (eds.), *Language Acquisition: Models and Methods*. London, Academic Press

Ireson, J. and Shields, M. (1985) Visual versus verbal clues in the recognition of emotion by children. Unpublished manuscript, University of London, Institute of Education

Jaffe, S. and Feldstein, S. (1970) *Rhythms of Dialogue*. New York, Academic Press

Karmiloff-Smith, A. (1979) *A Functional Approach to Child Language*. Cambridge, Cambridge University Press

Kaye, K. and Charney, R. (1981) Conversational asymmetry between mothers and children. *Journal of Child Language*, 8: 35–49

Keasy, P. (1979) Children's developing awareness and usage of intentionality and motives. In C. Blake Keasey (ed.), *Motivation*, Nebraska Symposium on Motivation. Nebraska City, University of Nebraska Press

Keenan, E. O. (1974) Conversational competence in children. *Journal of Child Language*, 1, 2: 163–83

(1976) The universality of conversational postulates. *Language and Society*, 5: 67–79

(1977) Making it last: repetition in children's discourse. In S. Ervin-Tripp and C. Mitchell-Kernan (eds.), *Child Discourse*. New York, Academic Press

Keenan, E. O. and Klein, E. (1975) Coherency in children's discourse. *Journal of Psycholinguistic Research*, 4: 365–78

Keenan, E. O. and Schieffelin, B. (1976) Topic as a discourse notion. In C. Li (ed.), *Subject and Topic*. New York, Academic Press

Langer, S. (1965) *Philosophy in a New Key*. Cambridge, MA, Harvard University Press

Levin, S. (1976) Concerning what kind of a poem a speech-act is. In T. van Dijk (ed.), *Pragmatics of Language and Literature*. Amsterdam, North Holland

Levine, L. and Hoffman, M. (1975) Empathy and cooperation in 4 year olds. *Developmental Psychology*, 11: 53–4

Levinson, S. C. (1981) The essential inadequacies of speech. Act models of dialogue. In H. Parret, M. Sbisā and J. Verschueren (eds.), *Possibilities and Limitations of Pragmatics*, Proceedings of the Conference on Pragmatics,

Urbino, 8–14 July 1979. Amsterdam, Benjamins

(1983) *Pragmatics*. Cambridge, Cambridge University Press

Light, P. (1979) *The Development of Social Sensitivity*. Cambridge, Cambridge University Press

McDonald, L. and Pien, D. (1982) Mother's conversational behaviour as a function of interactional intent. *Journal of Child Language*, 9: 337–58

McNeill, D. (1970a) *The Acquisition of Language: The Study of Developmental Psycholinguistics*. New York, Harper and Row

(1970b) The development of language. In P. H. Mussen (ed.), *Carmichael's Manual of Child Language*, vol. 1, New York, Wiley

McShane, J. (1980) *Learning to Talk*. Cambridge, Cambridge University Press

McTear, M. (1978) Repetition in child language: imitation or creation? In R. N. Campbell and P. T. Smith (eds.), *Recent Advances in the Psychology of Language: Language Development and Mother–Child Interaction*. New York and London, Plenum Press

(1985) *Children's Conversations*. Oxford, Blackwell

Masangkay, Z., McCluskey, K., McIntyre, C., Sims-Knight, J., Vaughan, B. and Flavell, J. (1974) The early development of inferences about the visual percepts of others. *Child Development*, 45: 357–66

Miller, P. H., Kessel, F. S. and Flavell, J. H. (1970) Thinking about people thinking about people thinking about . . . A study of social cognitive development. *Child Development*, 41: 613–23

Mitchell-Kernan, C. and Kernan, K. (1977) Pragmatics of directive choice among children. In S. Ervin-Tripp and C. Mitchell-Kernan (eds.), *Child Discourse*. New York, Academic Press

Morris, C. (1946) *Signs, Language and Behavior*. Englewood Cliffs, NJ, Prentice Hall

Nelson, K. (1973) Structure and strategy in learning to talk. In *Monographs of the Society of Research in Child Development*, 38, 1–2. Chicago, Chicago University Press

(1981) Social cognition in a script framework. In J. H. Flavell and L. Ross (eds.), *Social Cognitive Development*. Cambridge, Cambridge University Press

Nelson, K., Rescola, L., Grundel, J. and Benedict, H. (1978) Early lexicons: What do they mean? *Child Development*, 49: 960–8

Nigl, A. and Fishbein, H. (1974) Perception and conception in coordination of perspectives. *Developmental Psychology*, 10: 858–66

Ochs, E. (1979) What child language can contribute to pragmatics. In E. Ochs and B. Schieffelin (eds.), *Developmental Pragmatics*. New York, Academic Press

Olsen-Fulero, L. (1983) Acquiring language in a conversational context. *Journal of Child Language*, 10: 223–9

Peterson, C. L., Danner, E. W. and Flavell, J. H. (1972) Developmental changes in children's responses to three indications of communicative failure. *Child Development*, 43: 1463–8

Piaget, J. (1959) *The Language and Thought of the Child*. London, Routledge and Kegan Paul

Piaget, J. and Inhelder, B. (1956) *The Child's Conception of Space*. London, Routledge and Kegan Paul

Pomerantz, A. (1983) Agreeing and disagreeing in assessments: some features of preferred/dispreferred turn shapes. In J. M. Atkinson and J. Heritage, *Structures of Social Action*. Cambridge, Cambridge University Press

Prinz, P. (1983) The development of idiomatic meaning in children. *Language and Speech*, 26: 263–72

Rodgon, M. M. (1979) Knowing what to say and wanting to say it: some communicative and structural aspects of single word responses to questions. *Journal of Child Language*, 6: 81–91

Rosenberg, S. W. (1988) *Reason, Ideology and Politics*. Princeton, Princeton University Press

Sacks, H., Schegloff, E. A. and Jefferson, G. (1974) A simplest systematics for the organization of turn-taking in conversation. *Language*, 50, 4: 696–735

Searle, J. R. (1969) *Speech-Acts*. Cambridge, Cambridge University Press
    (1975) Indirect speech-acts. In Cole, P. and Morgan, J. L. (eds.), *Syntax and Semantics*, vol. 3, *Speech-Acts*. New York, Academic Press
    (1976) The classification of illocutionary acts. *Language and Society*, 5: 1–24
    (1979) *Expression and Meaning*. Cambridge, Cambridge University Press.

Shantz, C. U. (1975) The development of social cognition. In E. Hetherington (ed.), *Review of Child Development Research*, vol. 5. Chicago, University of Chicago Press
    (1982) Children's understanding of social rules and the social context. In F. C. Serafica (ed.), *Social Cognitive Development in Context*. New York, Guilford Press

Shantz, C. U. and Watson, J. (1971) Spatial abilities and spatial egocentrism in the young child. *Child Development*, 42: 171–81

Shatz, M. (1975) How young children respond to language: procedures for answering. In *Papers and Reports on Child Language Development*, 10. Stanford, Stanford University Press
    (1978) Children's comprehension of their mother's question-directives. *Journal of Child Language*, 5: 39–46

Shatz, M. and Gelman, R. (1973) *The Development of Communicative Skills: Modifications in the Speech of Young Children as a Function of Listener*. Monographs of the Society of Research in Child Development, 38, 5. Chicago, University of Chicago Press

Shields, M. (1985) The representation of emotions. Unpublished paper distributed at the Institute of Education, University of London

Shotter, J. (1980) Action, joint action and intentionality. In M. Brenner (ed.), *The Structure of Action*. Oxford, Blackwell

Snow, C. E. (1972) Mother's speech to children learning language. *Child Development*, 43: 549–65

(1977) The development of conversations between mothers and babies. *Journal of Child Language*, 4: 1–22

Spilton, D. and Lee, L. C. (1977) Some determinants of effective communication in 4 year olds. *Child Development*, 48: 968–77

StClair, R. N. and Giles, H. (1980) *The Social and Psychological Context of Language*, Hillsdale, NJ, Lawrence Erlbaum

Stefferson, M. S. (1978) Satisfying inquisitive adults: some simple methods of answering yes/no questions. *Journal of Child Language*, 5: 221–36

Strawson, P. F. (1964) Intention and convention in speech-acts. *Philosophical Review*, 73: 439–60

Sugarman-Bell, S. (1978) Some organizational aspects of pre-verbal communication. In I. Markova (ed.), *The Social Context of Language*. New York, Wiley

Tipton, I. C. (1977) *Locke on Human Understanding: Selected Essays*. Oxford, Oxford University Press

Turiel, E. (1978) The development of concepts of social structure: social convention. In J. Glick and A. Clarke-Stewart (eds.), *The Development of Social Understanding*, New York, Gardner Press

Vosniadou, S., Ortony, A., Reynolds, R. and Wilson, T. (1984) Sources of difficulty in the young child's understanding of metaphoric language. *Child Development*, 55: 1588–1606

Wells, G. (1986) Language, learning and teaching: helping learners to make knowledge their own. In F. Lowenthal and F. Vandame (eds.), *Pragmatics and Education*. New York and London, Plenum Press

Werth, P. (1981) *Conversation and Discourse: Structure and Interpretation*. London, Croom Helm

Winner, E., Engel, M., and Gardner, H. (1980) Misunderstanding metaphor: What's the problem? *Journal of Experimental Child Psychology*, 3: 22–32

Wittgenstein, L. (1958) *Philosophical Investigations*. Oxford, Blackwell

Author index

Subject index